Praise for *People Raising*

"I believe this is one of the most important and practical books in the history of world missions. I hope those who believe God's Word will read it and distribute it widely. It's not optional."

> GEORGE VERWER,
> *founder of Operation Mobilisation*

"Bill Dillon has a skillful way to motivate, train, and inspire people to overcome the natural fears associated with fundraising so they can accomplish the ministry God has given to them. It's filled with practical tips and coaching. When I led a mission organization that depended upon candidates raising their financial support, we found *People Raising* to be the best resource on the market."

> J. PAUL NYQUIST
> *president of Moody Bible Institute*

"Bill Dillon faithfully serves ministry leaders through his book *People Raising* and the principles taught in it. While God-centered ministries need to fully understand the art of raising funds, God's people also need to joyfully give as an act of their faith and obedience. I recommend this resource for leaders and laymen alike who wish to better understand how to do so."

> WESS STAFFORD
> *president and CEO of Compassion International*

"Whether raising funds as an individual or for your organization big or small, my friend Bill Dillon shows you how to build a relationship with your prospects and donors and develop a fundraising plan. Draw on his forty years of experience—and watch the Lord expand your ministry!"

> JOSEPH M. STOWELL
> *president of Cornerstone University*

D1055955

"Bill, thank you for this biblical approach to fundraising. Anyone raising their own financial support will be encouraged as they see these proven methods help them excel at funding their ministry."

JOSH MCDOWELL
author and speaker

"Church planters need funds but almost always are afraid of raising money. Bill Dillon's book, *People Raising*, helps take away the fear and provides the right steps. If you are planting a church and raising funds, you need this resource."

ED STETZER
president of LifeWay Research

"The end goal of fundraising is not the money. It is about inviting people to participate in kingdom work through their generosity. Bill Dillon has done an incredible service for the kingdom by addressing both the spiritual aspect of raising funds and the required skills in his excellent book, *People Raising*."

ELLIS F. GOLDSTEIN
director, ministry partner development, Campus Crusade for Christ

"Bill Dillon's expanded version of *People Raising* will both inform and inspire the would-be fundraiser to achieve greater levels of effectiveness through proper backgrounding, improved strategies, and better approaches. There's a great new section for fundraising coaches and new material on social media today. Bill's principles have already helped our organization grow more rapidly than we could have grown otherwise."

DOUG LUCAS
founder of Brigada Today *and president of Team Expansion*

"*People Raising* is a must read for all those charged with fundraising responsibilities. While the book is geared for individuals, the principles apply to everyone required to raise financial support. Bill Dillon does a masterful job combining biblical foundation with a practical approach."

TAMI HEIM
president and CEO of the Christian Leadership Alliance

"Bill Dillon has done more for raising personal support than anyone I know, and this book is essential reading for anyone who feels called to ministry. It will provide a biblical basis, a sound strategy, and practical examples of how to approach the joy of sharing ministry. After all, as Bill so clearly states, the support you are asking for is not about you, it's to advance the kingdom."

DOUG SHAW

chairman and CEO of Douglas Shaw & Associates, fundraising counsel

"At Stadia we always recommend Bill Dillon and the tried and true teaching of *People Raising*. Our goal is to plant 100 churches a year. *People Raising* will make this possible."

THOMAS F. JONES Jr.

executive director of Stadia: Together We Will

"*People Raising* is a must read for any church planter. It addresses the 'elephant in the room'—money! And, it does it in a practical, simple, and biblically sound fashion."

NICK BORING

U.S. Catalyst, Vision360

"Financial support for ministry needs to be 'mined' in a biblical and God-honoring way, coupled with the right attitude. This biblically based practical guide to fundraising directs one into doing just that."

MARVIN NEWELL

executive director of CrossGlobal Link

"Bill provides a great balance between the priority of dependence on God's provision and the necessity of an organized, intentional approach. Thank you, Bill, for providing such a valuable tool!"

DON PARROTT

president and CEO of Finishers Project

"Raising personal support requires the development of new skills for the missionary. *People Raising* is a wealth of practical principles, steps, and ideas for cultivating those skills. Bill Dillon provides an excellent aid for both the individual missionary and those who coach missionaries in support-raising."

DAVE BLOMBERG

director of ministry partnership, Mission Aviation Fellowship

"Here's a valuable and comprehensive resource and reference for people in partnership ministry. I don't think I've seen a book that covers the topic as thoroughly. I will be recommending it for the faith ministry workers coming through the partnership training and coaching process of Kingdom Come Training."

JERRY LONG

president of Kingdom Come Training

"In *People Raising*, Bill Dillon provides a proven recipe and practical steps regarding the what to do: raising the people and funds essential to kingdom work. The systematic application of his insights will yield multiple dividends to you and your ministry for years to come."

LARRY F. JOHNSTON

president of McConkey • Johnston International

"All fund raising, large or small, is the management of relationships. Bill gets that and his new updated book is well worth the read for those who love people and love to see their ministries grow."

PATRICK MCLAUGHLIN

president and founder of The Timothy Group

"This new edition provides a whole new generation of church planters with a wealth of wisdom, practical ideas, and doable action plans. This isn't just a book you read, this is a book you do."

CRAIG WHITNEY

director of Emerging Leadership Initiative

People Raising

A Practical Guide to Raising Funds

WILLIAM P. DILLON

MOODY PUBLISHERS

CHICAGO

All scripture quotations, unless otherwise indicated, are taken from the *Holy Bible, New International Version*®, NIV®. Copyright © 1973, 1978, 1984 by Biblica, Inc.™ Used by permission of Zondervan. All rights reserved worldwide. www.zondervan.com.

Scripture quotations marked NKJV are taken from the *New King James Version*. Copyright © 1982 by Thomas Nelson, Inc. Used by permission. All rights reserved.

Scripture quotations marked THE MESSAGE are from *The Message,* copyright © by Eugene H. Peterson 1993, 1994, 1995. Used by permission of NavPress Publishing Group.

All websites and phone numbers listed herein are accurate at the time of publication but may change in the future or cease to exist. The listing of website references and resources does not imply publisher endorsement of the site's entire contents. Groups and organizations are listed for informational purposes, and listing does not imply publisher endorsement of their activities.

Edited by: Annette LaPlaca
Interior design: Smartt Guys design
Cover design: Garborg Design Works
Cover image: Shutterstock 25417945 | Bigstock 18832172

Library of Congress Cataloging-in-Publication Data

Dillon, William P. (William Paul)
 People raising : a practical guide to raising funds for individuals and organizations / William P. Dillon.
    p. cm.
 Includes bibliographical references (p.   ).
 ISBN 978-0-8024-6448-4
 1. Church finance. 2. Fund raising. I. Title.
 BV772.5.D55 2012
 254'.8–dc23

                        2011050520

We hope you enjoy this book from Moody Publishers. Our goal is to provide high-quality, thought-provoking books and products that connect truth to your real needs and challenges. For more information on other books and products written and produced from a biblical perspective, go to www.moodypublishers.com or write to:

Moody Publishers
820 N. LaSalle Boulevard
Chicago, IL 60610

3 5 7 9 10 8 6 4 2

Printed in the United States of America

To my wife, Sandy, who joined me in 1972
on a journey of faith as we began Inner City Impact
on a sidewalk—with no meeting place, no staff,
and no financial support.
But the vision was alive in both our hearts.

To my son Brian, his wife, Cessandra,
my granddaughters Eddie, Faith, and
precious Abigail, who is present with the Lord.

To my daughter, Christina, her husband, Kevin,
my grandson Shane, and granddaughter Ruby.

To my son Bradley, his wife, Rachel,
and my grandsons, Nate and Ben.

I love you all very much.

CONTENTS

Implementing Your Fundraising Plan

PREFACE

One of the obstacles standing in the way of Christians fulfilling the Great Commission is the dwindling supply of Christian workers. Without an expanding workforce, we will be unable to deliver the gospel. Often what prevents willing servants from getting down to the work they long to do is a lack of effective strategy for raising funds.

The phone in my office rings at Inner City Impact in Chicago. When I answer, the voice on the other end fires off a series of questions. The speaker seems eager to be involved in our cause of bringing hope through the gospel to the children of the inner city. Finally he asks, "Do I have to raise my financial support?"

When I respond affirmatively, the questioning abruptly ends, and another potential candidate is blown off the scene. He has heard horror stories about raising funds and doesn't want to go through the hassle others are forced to endure.

Several months later another phone call comes. A pastor relates that a respected evangelical mission approved a member of his congregation for missionary service. The prospective missionary had been raising funds for eighteen months but is not even close to meeting their financial goal. The prospective missionary, disappointed, has withdrawn from ministry.

These Christians with a passion for the gospel and a vision for growing God's kingdom become frustrated into giving up before they can fully begin! Even more disturbing is the number of potential staff who never consider missions or church planting because they hear negative stories about fundraising. They need to hear positive stories of those who have succeeded in raising the needed funds in a timely fashion, who have made it to their assignments, and who are engaged in ministry.

There is help and hope for ministry workers facing the challenges of fundraising. Nearly twenty years ago, the first edition of *People Raising* came together with the collected wisdom of experienced fundraisers. For years I studied the efforts of missions and organizations to raise funds. Very few had effective strategies. I asked more than one hundred mission organizations to send me the materials they used to prepare missionary candidates. I also asked them to direct me to other missions that seemed to have a good handle on fundraising. In some cases, I got what I expected: very little. In other cases, I was pleasantly surprised. The information I gathered, along with lessons learned through my own experience, went into the first edition of this book.

Today I continue to raise funds and train others. As we prepared to update *People Raising*, it became in many senses almost a complete rewrite. I know you will enjoy and benefit from the insights and experiences I have discovered that will make you even more effective. I count it a privilege to come alongside ministry workers with encouragement for this important ministry of fundraising that we call People Raising.

My goal continues to be to reduce the fear and time it takes for prospective or veteran missionaries, church planters, and Christian organizations to raise prayer and financial support.

You will discover a purposeful strategy here. But recognize that our dependence is not on systems and strategies, but on the Lord. I am reminded that Psalm 147:10–11 says, "His pleasure is not in the strength of the horse, nor his delight in the legs of a man; the Lord delights in those who fear him, who put their hope in his unfailing love." I will walk you through a well-designed system that has been proved and tested. But I am humbled as I watch the Lord work far beyond my human efforts.

With our hope rightly placed in a holy and awesome God, we can't go wrong. It is my prayer that the following material will help both the Christian worker and the ministry as they endeavor to fulfill the Great Commission.

HOW TO USE THIS BOOK

Various people in the Christian community will glean from this book and use it as a tool to sharpen their fundraising skills:

- Church planter
- New or veteran missionary
- President of a nonprofit organization
- Director of development of a nonprofit organization
- Mission personnel director or candidate secretary
- Mission professor looking for a textbook on fundraising
- College placement personnel who counsel summer and career missionaries
- Member of a church missions committee
- Pastoral staff member who guides missionaries in fundraising
- Concerned Christian looking to pass on practical resources to Christian workers

I advise reading through the book to grasp the total strategy before implementing the recommended steps. The book is designed to take you step by step in this exciting journey of raising funds for the Lord's work. Each step builds on the previous step, and the whole process will begin to make sense. Don't take shortcuts! I will never forget the person who walked up to me during a break at a conference in St. Louis. He had a number of questions about *People Raising*, and as we were talking, another person walked over and began to listen to our conversation.

The second man interrupted and said, "I've been through Bill's materials and when he says write a letter, write a letter. When he says make a call, make a call. When he says to sit down with a prospective donor, sit down with that person. Follow what Bill has to say and you won't go wrong." There will be many occasions when I will challenge you to move outside your comfort zone, but realize that thousands of people have been trained effectively through *People*

Raising. Don't let fear paralyze you!

The training content is primarily geared to individuals raising funds. If you are raising funds for an organization, the very same principles can be applied. Whether you are asking for $100 a month for personal support or asking $25,000 for a project for your organization, the same process and principles apply. I look to you to make those adjustments as you read.

There are more People Raising tools beyond the book. You can access the People Raising website and purchase our training program in DVD, CD, or MP3. This is loaded with practical examples of fundraising, questions from the audience, more than a hundred PowerPoint slides, and role-playing. You can order these online at www.peopleraising.com. Then our live seminar will take your fundraising to the next level. It will go a long way to reduce the fear and time it takes to raise needed funds.

Cultivating a
POSITIVE ATTITUDE
toward
FUNDRAISING

CHAPTER 1

The Benefits of Raising Funds

Many people who are called to be missionaries are given the assignment to raise funds, and yet the reality is they have never raised funds before. So it is fair to ask the question, "Why raise financial support?" I want to unveil for you the benefits of raising funds—and there are many.

Maybe you are considering missionary service or church planting, or maybe you have already been involved in ministry. In either case, the question, "Why raise financial support?" is a crucial one for you.

I grew up in a missionary home, where I saw faith at work. I attended Moody Bible Institute and heard every conceivable missionary message. I talked with many missionaries and read missionary biographies. However, it was not until I personally raised funds for our ministry that I comprehended the important reasons for developing a base of consecrated supporters. After nearly forty years, I have come to understand that raising financial support is necessary for many reasons.

Raising Financial Support Attracts a Base of Prayer Support

If you worked on our staff at Inner City Impact in a salaried position, few people would commit themselves to pray for you. However, when you serve in a missionary capacity, the people who invest financially in you are inclined to pray for you. Prayer follows financial investment.

Raising Financial Support Stretches Your Faith

To those about to begin raising funds, David Tucker of Regions Beyond Missionary Union International says: "You are about to embark on what can be one of the most maturing and spiritually fulfilling ventures of your life."

Raising financial support stretches your faith.

Raising financial support can be a spiritual adventure. You'll love many aspects of it. But we rarely grow and mature by doing what is easy. When friends you expected to give do not, it's discouraging. When days go by and your level of support does not increase, you may be tempted to question your call. Those are the days when you step forward in faith, trusting that God has called you and that in His time He will supply every need. Raising financial support will teach you what it means to walk by faith.

Raising Financial Support Stimulates and Encourages Vision in the Body of Christ

Raising financial support calls for the missionary or church planter to interface with other believers who make up the body of Christ. When Christians meet face-to-face, they communicate Christ's vision, His call. Another person's enthusiasm and dedication will stimulate your interest and involvement in kingdom work.

In his article "The Tin-Cup Image Can Be Shattered," Daniel Bacon describes the missionary who raises financial support as accomplishing three goals.

First, *the missionary is a model for missions.* That may seem scary, but you must never forget God has given you your status. In essence, you are a walking testimony of God's coveted plan for world evangelism. Bacon says, "The presence of a missionary is a living illustration of obedience to the Great Commission." In raising support, you keep God's priority of ministry in front of the body of Christ and help others become mission-minded.

Second, *the missionary becomes a mobilizer for kingdom work.* You provide believers the opportunity to participate in God's program for world evangelism financially and through prayer. Because of your deputation ministry, some may sense God's heart for mission and join the workforce.

Third, *the missionary serves as a minister for missions and ministry.* You facilitate effective communication that will bring together the mission agency and the local church. Bacon says, "The missionary obviously needs the church for support, but the church needs the missionary to extend, in obedience to the Great Commission, its ministry worldwide."[1] We will talk more about opportunities to minister later in the book.

Raising Financial Support Broadens the Base of Financial Support for Your Organization

If your organization were to hire staff members based on their financial resources, you would have only a handful of staff. Rather, the organization counts on the staff member through his network of people to broaden its financial base. When your friends support you financially, you play an integral part in broadening your organization's financial base.

Raising Financial Support Develops You as a Person

Bud Taylor of Source of Light Ministries, International, offers this perspective:

> There are many things that God will teach you that you could not possibly learn anywhere else. You learn how to work with people and how to adapt under divergent, difficult, and sometimes desperate circumstances. That is when the realization dawns that we are so limited and God is so limitless! It is not as is so often misrepresented a punitive measure, but a privilege. It is not a promotional gimmick, but a prerequisite. In the process one learns poise, polish, and proficiency and how to use time, tact, and talent to [one's] best advantage.[2]

Raising Financial Support Stimulates Fellowship among Other Believers

As you contact your network of people and add friends to that network, you become involved with caring, praying, and burdened people. Rewarding times of fellowship result as you interact with believers through the fundraising process.

Raising Financial Support Opens Opportunities to Witness

As you travel from place to place, making new contacts, God gives divine appointments with the unsaved world. And through those opportunities, you begin to participate in others' call to fulfill the Great Commission.

Scott Steele and Tom Frieze of International Missions say, "Missions was and is God's idea, and it is a real privilege to speak to God's people about God's program and to enlist their petitions."[3]

Raising financial support is far more than raising money. It is ministry. It is relationships. It is watching God work His eternal program for the ages in a practical way.

CHAPTER 2

The Biblical Basis for Raising Funds

As you consider raising funds, you may wonder whether raising financial support is biblical. Does Scripture say anything about the process? Are there principles, commands, dos or don'ts, or any models in the Bible?

I guarantee you: The Scriptures are not silent about finances.

Jesus spoke often concerning wealth—its use and its careless abuse. In fact, He spoke more directly about stewardship than about any other subject. Approximately seven hundred direct statements in the Bible relate to finances. One could add a hundred more indirect references. Nearly two-thirds of the parables of Christ deal with the use of wealth. God often relates our use of wealth with our commitment to Him.[1]

Teaching materials from SIM (Serving In Mission) point out, "A review of Scripture reveals an amazing amount of material related to this subject." The material that follows is adapted from SIM's "introduction to an interesting and valuable personal study."[2]

The Old Testament Pattern

Scripture supports the idea that God is ultimately in charge of providing for His people, and your experience in fundraising will show you times when God provides miraculously—beyond any strategy or efforts of your own. Remember how God fed His people, the Israelites, while they wandered in the wilderness, with the miraculous provision of quail and manna to eat (Exodus 16:13–17; Joshua 5:12), or how God provided for His servant Elijah by sending ravens with bread and meat (1 Kings 17:1–6). God can and does provide

The Scriptures are not silent about finances.

miraculously sometimes.

But God put a structure in place for the support of ministry workers. Numbers 18:21–24 lays out the Old Testament pattern for support. God called for the nation of Israel to give a tithe to support their "full-time" spiritual leaders. God never changed the plan, and the Old Testament ends with a stern rebuke to the nation for not giving these tithes (Malachi 3:8). This was God's plan, not something Moses or Aaron dreamed up.

> "I give to the Levites all the tithes in Israel as their inheritance in return for the work they do while serving at the Tent of Meeting. From now on the Israelites must not go near the Tent of Meeting, or they will bear the consequences of their sin and will die. It is the Levites who are to do the work at the Tent of Meeting and bear the responsibility for offenses against it. This is a lasting ordinance for the generations to come. They will receive no inheritance among the Israelites. Instead, I give to the Levites as their inheritance the tithes that the Israelites present as an offering to the Lord. That is why I said concerning them: 'They will have no inheritance among the Israelites.'" (Numbers 18:21–24)

God's tithing system is restated in Deuteronomy 14:22–29, stipulating that a portion of the tithe is intended to cover the Levites (full-time ministry workers). In 2 Chronicles 31:4, Hezekiah the king orders his subjects who lived in Jerusalem to provide for the priests and the Levites, so they could devote themselves to God's law.

You'll recall also that God called on His people to provide for the creation of the Tabernacle (Exodus 25–31, 35–40) and for the building of the temple (1 Chronicles 29; 2 Chronicles 2; 2 Chronicles 4:4-22; Ezra 1).

God's plan was that the people as a group should provide for those in ministry, and leaders regularly called on God's people to make that provision.

The New Testament Pattern

In Luke 8:1–3, we see the pattern for support illustrated in Jesus' ministry. He allowed others to minister to Him physically and materially. He was not embarrassed to receive help as they gave to Him of their substances (goods, possessions, and property). These verses include the statement that "The

Twelve were with him" (Luke 8:1). The implication is that Jesus and His disciples were giving themselves fully to ministering to people, and the people were providing for their needs.

> After this, Jesus traveled about from one town and village to another, proclaiming the good news of the kingdom of God. The Twelve were with him, and also some women who had been cured of evil spirits and diseases: Mary (called Magdalene) from whom seven demons had come out; Johanna the wife of Cuza, the manager of Herod's household; Susanna; and many others. These women were helping to support them out of their own means. (Luke 8:1–3)

The Twelve were sent out by direction from Jesus, not by their own choice or volition (Matthew 10:5). They were to give themselves fully to ministry, not to earning a living. They were not allowed to take food or money for operating expenses. Rather, they were to depend on God's supply, and God's plan for that provision was through other people (Matthew 10:5–15).

Christ allowed others to minister to Him.

God's Plan Calls for Christian Workers To Share Their Needs

The disciples were instructed to inquire who in the city was worthy of God's blessing (Matthew 10:11). Apparently they were to request hospitality from one of those families. The implication is that God was going to bless the home that provided hospitality because of the disciples' presence. But the disciples had to be bold to the point of actually asking for lodging.

In his letter to the Romans, Paul clearly states that he expects fellow Christians to help him on his way to Spain to preach the gospel. There appears to be no hesitation in his statement: "I plan to do so when I go to Spain. I hope to visit you while passing through and to have you assist me on my journey there, after I have enjoyed your company for a while" (Romans 15:24).

Paul makes another direct request for financial help from a church in 2 Corinthians 1:15–16: "Because I was confident of this, I planned to visit you first so that you might benefit twice. I planned to visit you on my way to Macedonia and to come back to you from Macedonia, and then to have you send me on my way to Judea." (See also 1 Corinthians 16:6 and Philippians 4:10–20.)

In the Old Testament, the prophet Elijah was bold to ask for the last bit of food a widow had. Elijah based his request on his confident trust that God would reward the woman's faith. The result was God's provision for Elijah's need and His great blessing on the widow and her son.

> The word of the Lord came to [Elijah]: "Go at once to Zarephath of Sidon and stay there. I have commanded a widow in that place to supply you with food." So he went to Zarephath. When he came to the town gate, a widow was there gathering sticks. He called to her and asked, "Would you bring me a little water in a jar so I may have a drink?" As she was going to get it, he called, "And bring me, please, a piece of bread."
>
> "As surely as the Lord your God lives," she replied, "I don't have any bread—only a handful of flour in a jar and a little oil in a jug. I am gathering a few sticks to take home and make a meal for myself and my son, that we may eat it—and die."
>
> Elijah said to her, "Don't be afraid. Go home and do as you have said. But first make a small cake of bread for me from what you have and bring it to me, and then make something for yourself and your son. For this is what the Lord, the God of Israel, says: 'The jar of flour will not be used up and the jug of oil will not run dry until the day the Lord gives rain on the land.'"
>
> She went away and did as Elijah had told her. So there was food every day for Elijah and for the woman and her family. For the jar of flour was not used up and the jug of oil did not run dry, in keeping with the word of the Lord spoken by Elijah. (1 Kings 17:8–16)

SIM makes the following statement regarding raising funds.

> If the Lord has called you into full-time Christian ministry, it is His plan that you be supported by other Christians except in unusual cases. It is His plan, not just your plan or your organization's plan.
>
> Support raising is a ministry. It is not begging people for money. Rather, it is an opportunity for you to share your vision . . . People must be challenged to have a part in the Great Commission through you.
>
> Support raising provides opportunity for blessing to those who give to you. And God gives them credit for your fruit.

Not that I am looking for a gift, but I am looking for what may be credited to your account. I have received full payment and even more; I am amply supplied, now that I have received from Epaphroditus the gifts you sent. They are a fragrant offering, an acceptable sacrifice, pleasing to God. And my God will meet all your needs according to his glorious riches in Christ Jesus. (Philippians 4:17–19)

For the sake of the gospel, it is appropriate to share our specific needs with those capable of helping us. Thus, support raising systems do not detract from trusting God as the source of the supply of your need.[3]

Clearly Scripture is not silent about finances. Through the centuries, God has supplied His people's needs through others. You can be confident that He has promised to supply your every need as well (Philippians 4:19).

That raises more questions: Do we tell people our needs? Do we ask for support? Or do we wait in full faith that God will direct others to meet our needs without our revealing those needs? We will address these questions in the next chapter as we study the convictions of God's great heroes of faith.

For Further Study

1. Read the following verses compiled by the Navigators on biblical fundraising. Write principles or observations about fundraising from each verse.

Exodus 25:1–2; 35:4–5 _____

_____

_____

Numbers 8:14; 18:21–24 _____

_____

_____

Deuteronomy 14:27; 16:17 _____

_____

_____

1 Samuel 9:7–8 _____

_____

_____

1 Kings 17:1–16 _____

_____

_____

Nehemiah 2:1–8; 13:14 _____

_____

_____

Proverbs 30:7–9 _____

_____

_____

Matthew 10:5–15 _____

_____

_____

Luke 8:1–3; 10:1–8; 16:10–12; 21:1–4; 22:35–38 _____

_____

_____

John 12:3–8 _____

_____

_____

Acts 10:2–4; 18:3–5; 20:33–35 _____

_____

_____

Romans 15:20–24 _____

_____

_____

2 Corinthians 1:16; 8–9; 12:13 _____

_____

_____

Galatians 6:6 _____

_____

_____

Philippians 4:10–20_____

_____

_____

1 Thessalonians 2:9 _____

_____

_____

2 Thessalonians 3:7–9_____

_____

_____

1 Timothy 5:17–18; 6:17 _____

_____

_____

2. What does Scripture have to say about the biblical basis for the Christian
   worker's being supported by others, based on Numbers 18:21–24, Matthew
   10:5–15, Luke 8:1–3, Acts 18:3–5, and 1 Corinthians 9? _____

_____

_____

_____

3. Describe the biblical basis for soliciting or making needs known, based on
   1 Kings 17, Matthew 10:11, Romans 15:24, and 2 Corinthians 1:16. _____

_____

_____

_____

CHAPTER 3

Yes, It Is Okay to Ask for Funds

Now that we have firmly established that it is biblical to raise funds, you might still wonder if it is right to ask for funds. To ask or not to ask? That is the question.

Many people turn to the example of missionary George Mueller, who ran his ministry by prayer and prayer alone, with no solicitation whatsoever. Joel Darby gives us some helpful insights in these excerpts from his article called "Why Not Do It Like George Mueller?"

> Someone asked me the other day why we did not support Book Fellowship soul-winning enterprises as George Mueller did with his orphanages—tell no one but God about the needs. This person could not have realized that this had been my heartfelt dream in the early days of the work, for I am an ardent admirer of Mueller and his great work. . . .
>
> We worked and waited and prayed, but the needed funds did not come in. We searched our hearts for anything that could hold back answers to prayer. . . .
>
> Then one day we read of some early experiences of Dwight L. Moody, who has left an even more monumental work behind him than Mueller. (Many thousands of young people, still going to the mission fields of the world.)
>
> I was shocked to learn that Moody made no bones of declaring the needs, even to slapping a Christian businessman on the back and

suggesting he invest a few thousand dollars in precious souls! Who am I to say he was NOT led of God when he did it? . . .

We came to realize, finally, that God has His own plan for every organization He raises up, and it is up to us to find His will for our particular situation and follow it faithfully. . . .

Perhaps His most important reasons for not allowing us the quiet George Mueller method was to enlist thousands to earnestly PRAY for the work. God did not want to support this work by large amounts coming miraculously from unknown sources. He wanted thousands of people praying intelligently, each one becoming truly one of us in sacrifice and prayer for precious souls. We feel sure we followed His leading and will learn all His reasons up there.[1]

God Is Faithful

I personally have seen God work miracles as I've asked individuals to be involved financially in our ministry. And I have seen God expand our ministry. We started Inner City Impact on a sidewalk—with no staff, no place to meet, and, obviously, no finances. But we had a vision. Our desire was to bring hope to inner-city children, and I will never forget the first financial gifts we received from friends who believed in us and in our vision.

Soon we found an old union hall that miraculously became available free of charge. When God provided our own facility two years later, the challenge increased. We had to raise more funds to pay the mortgage, insurance, remodeling costs, and maintenance. It was my job to challenge people to give.

And God was faithful. People caught the vision, and new contacts were made. When God put them in front of me, I had to muster up the courage to invite them to be a part of the financial solution to our needs. The ministry has continued to grow until today we operate in three communities in Chicago. Every year God supplies hundreds of thousands of dollars to support the workers, facilities, and programs.

You, too, have needs, and God will send you chosen servants who are capable of giving. They need to be asked, and that is the role you play.

SIM provides more perspective on this issue of whether or not to ask in its material titled "A Miraculous Way to Function":

[First] we look to God for the provision of our needs. . . . It's a miraculous way to function. There is no human guarantee, no assurance of funds from any source. But God supplies. . . .

That leads to the second principle: we inform God's people of the needs. We do this because God meets these needs through His people. People are the channels He has ordained for accomplishing this purpose. . . .

Christian people need to give. It is part of the Christian experience, rooted in the fact that God gives to us. . . .

SIM is not looking merely for contributors—people who are not truly involved with us. We are looking for stewards who understand what biblical giving is. . . .

The final principle zeros in on our responsibility as the recipient of funds provided by God's stewards: *integrity in their use.* It is vitally important that we use such money as wisely and effectively as we know how.[2]

While it is one of our roles to find funds for ministry, naturally no one wants to be pegged as "a beggar." Don W. Hillis, of TEAM (The Evangelical Alliance Mission) writes about this helpfully in his article "Are Missionaries Beggars?".

"How to be sure of the will of God" has been replaced as the number one problem of Christian young people who are thinking of missions. The big hang-up now is money. They object to begging for support. . . .

In the Old Testament economy those who served the Lord and His people (the priests, Levites, and prophets) lived off the tithes and offerings of the people. And there was a definite relationship between Israel's faithfulness in giving and God's blessing upon the nation. The prophet Malachi accused Israel of robbing God in relation to tithes and offerings. He then promised that God would open "the floodgates of heaven" to those who would be faithful in the matter of giving (Malachi 3:8–10).

Jesus, who so easily could have turned stones into bread and who multiplied loaves and fishes, lived off the gifts of His friends during His public ministry. Then He pulled the economy rug out from under the feet of those He called into His service. He insisted that the fishermen should leave their fishing, the tax collector his tax collecting, and the tent maker his tent making. When Jesus sent out the seventy "into every city and place," He commanded them to "carry neither purse, nor script, nor shoes." They were to accept the hospitality of those who would open their homes, "eating and drinking such things as they give, for the laborer is worthy of his hire" (Luke 10:4–7).

The Lord has ordained that those who "preach the gospel should live from the gospel" (1 Corinthians 9:14 NKJV). And is a pastor expecting his people to support him any different from an apostle (missionary) expecting churches to support him? . . .

Dr. Fenton shares this wise counsel: "See yourself not as a huckster of your own services or as a promoter of your own support, but as one who has had firsthand contact with God—and who, therefore, has something to share with others. See your mission to the churches not as a money-raising junket, but as a further fulfillment of the great commission; you are going because of a divine call—to share with others what you know of Jesus Christ." When the missionary candidate sees raising of his support as an opportunity to prove his faith, to inform fellow Christians of God's work, to inspire them to invest in things of eternal consequence, and to encourage them to pray for him and for the work of the Lord, then his deputation is no longer a mountain but a ministry. He probably will even find himself making new personal friendships that will be of rich spiritual benefit to him, to his friends, and to his work. There is no substitute for friends who really care. . . .

Are missionaries beggars? I guess the answer really depends upon one's perspective of God's work and interpretation of His Word.[3]

> *Don't create your strategy based on convenience.*

Let me offer a word of caution. There are those who will readily walk away from fundraising merely because of fear or inconvenience. When you get down to it, they have arrived at their position not from a careful study of Scripture but out of convenience rather than conviction.

Be careful; it is easy to fall into that trap. As you keep reading, many of you will be challenged to move beyond your comfort zone. It will be easy to turn a deaf ear to the People Raising strategy and fall back on ineffective methods that seem more convenient. For example, it is a lot easier to send a letter than make a personal call and sit down with prospective donors. Accept the challenge! As you personally develop a fundraising plan that fits into God's purpose for you, He will enable you with confidence to proceed.

Three Models for Fundraising

There are basically three different fundraising models, and Christians can readily identify each with a well-known fundraising personality:

> **George Mueller: Prayer alone**
>
> **Hudson Taylor: Pray and inform**
>
> **D. L. Moody: Pray, inform, and ask**

George Sweeting, the sixth president of Moody Bible Institute, summarizes the three approaches to fundraising:

> In guiding a ministry, should one be aggressive in raising funds, or is it more biblical or spiritual to pray and wait upon God to act? That debate continues, but it appears for good or ill that aggressiveness has prevailed.
>
> D. L. Moody probably had something to do with the outcome of this controversy. This is especially clear when we compare Moody to some of his contemporaries, like George Mueller and Hudson Taylor.
>
> Mueller is the evangelical's prototype of the passivist. He worked in Bristol, England, and founded homes for orphans. His biographies are filled with stories of faith about how no one knew a particular need but God alone, and right when the need was most urgent, the money for which Mueller prayed miraculously came in.
>
> Regarding solicitation, Mueller said, "It is not enough to obtain means for the work of God, but that these means should be obtained in God's way. To ask unbelievers for means is not God's way. To press even believers to give is not God's way; but the duty and privilege of being allowed to contribute to the work of God should be pointed

out, and this should be followed up with earnest prayer, believing prayer, and will result in the desired end."

For Mueller, the key was in waiting on God for the annual 25,000 pounds to provide for his 200 children. He spent time praying that would ordinarily go to fundraising. He wanted to prove God's faithfulness. Once he even withheld the annual statement of his ministry, lest someone consider its information to be an appeal.

But Mueller did not inform the public about the progress of his work nor give account of how funds were used. All he asked of his supporters was to pray for God's provision. There was minimal information and no solicitation.

Hudson Taylor, founder of the China Inland Mission, was burdened to recruit workers for the missionary enterprise. Like Mueller, he made no appeals for money. He wanted to sustain the work by prayer alone. In an attitude that is almost incomprehensible in our own day, Taylor wanted to avoid diverting funds from older benevolent societies. Subscription lists were out.

"The apostolic plan," he said, "was not to raise ways and means but to go and do the work, trusting His promise who said, 'Seek ye first the kingdom of God and His righteousness and all these things shall be added unto you.'" God's work done in God's way would not lack God's supply.

For Taylor this meant that if there was a need, he would pray and tell others about the need. He was considerably more aggressive than Mueller in announcing his needs. For example, in the "First Occasional Paper" of the mission in 1866, the exact amount of the needs was specified in print.

So in practice, *Taylor went a step further than Mueller. He believed and practiced "full information, but no solicitation."*

Moody differed from these two evangelical giants . . . He said, "I show my faith when I go to men and state to them the needs of the Lord's work and ask them to give to it." And ask he did.

If Mueller practiced minimal information and no solicitation, and if Taylor stood for full information and no solicitation, then *Moody stood for both full information and, for the most part, full solicitation.* This aggressiveness was startling to some in the evangelical orbit. In fact, the

Moody Bible Institute today differs from its founder by sharing full information coupled with gentle, faithful solicitation. . . .

Moody's secret, said Lyman Abbott, another friend, was his "artless faith that all money belongs to the Lord, and that it can be had for the Lord's work if one goes about in the right way to get it."[4]

There is not a right or wrong model, and there is no single model. But I advise you not to build your philosophy out of convenience but to be willing to move out of your comfort zone.

What does that add up to? The fact that we are workers together, sharing our various resources—including money—to achieve goals for God. Fundraising can be viewed as a three-pronged relationship:

Each member of the relationship has a job description.

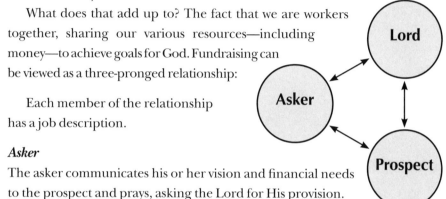

Asker

The asker communicates his or her vision and financial needs to the prospect and prays, asking the Lord for His provision.

Prospect

As a member of the body of Christ, the prospect ought to be willing to listen and be made aware of the asker's vision and needs. The prospective giver then ought to pray about the asker's request, asking God if a financial gift is His will.

Lord

God is responsible for providing finances for the asker, who has been given an assignment from the Lord. The Lord also will provide direction to the prospect on how he should give financially.

With this relationship in mind, the asker can share his vision with confidence and ask a prospective giver to participate financially while carefully bringing about a decision.

While growing up in the home of missionaries, I watched my mom and dad live lives of faith. When we were having a home built, we prayed at every phase, and we watched God provide.

As a student at Moody Bible Institute, I listened intently as ministry workers told their personal stories of faith, and I was intrigued. To fulfill class assignments, I read missionary biographies that described the excitement of living by faith. Yet I had never taken great steps of faith of my own.

When we began the ministry of Inner City Impact, I was confronted with the question of how to raise funds. I watched, studied, questioned, and hammered out what became my personal philosophy of raising funds. God led our family and our mission this way. For nearly forty years our needs have been met, and the entire ministry is debt-free.

CHAPTER 4

Confronting the Fear Factor

People Raising is designed to reduce the fear and time it takes to raise needed funds. That fear is real. But notice my wording: I wrote, "*reduce* the fear." I am not convinced I can eliminate the fear.

A perfect example goes back to the early days when I began Inner City Impact. I was fearful. We began our ministry in a community some referred to as one of the most dangerous communities in the country. But the more I engaged in the community and they engaged with me, the fear was reduced—but not eliminated.

Fundraising is the same way. The fear can be diminished, but not eliminated altogether.

InterVarsity's Donna Wilson understands fundraising. In a seminar titled "Overcoming Emotional Barriers in Fundraising," Wilson provides an excellent perspective in addressing the fear.

Wilson urges InterVarsity staffers to *identify the emotions*. Most often they come up with fear, shame, unworthiness, guilt, and embarrassment. She uses the following questions to help uncover the core beliefs that lead to these feelings:

Can you describe the situation making you feel fearful?
What do you think you are afraid of?
What do you believe you are guilty of?
In what way is it shameful to be raising funds?
Why do you feel you don't deserve to be supported?[1]

Reduce the fear of fundraising.

Experience has convinced Donna Wilson that most of these negative emotions stem from inaccurate beliefs, often subconsciously absorbed from cultural messages or from lies about ourselves we are tempted to accept. Wilson uses God's Word to correct the inaccurate beliefs:

Beliefs about money and possessions

Inaccurate belief: *I'm asking people to give me some of their money.*

Biblical view: *I'm inviting people to give back to God some of His resources for His work (1 Chronicles 29:14–16).*

Beliefs about personal worth

Inaccurate belief: *My value lies in what I own or accomplish; my worth is reflected by my position and salary.*

Biblical view: *Our value comes from God and His love for us. We are friends, children, and heirs of the King (Romans 8:14–17).*

Beliefs about giving

Inaccurate belief: *Giving is a nice thing to do but can only be done after people have met their own needs/wants* **OR** *Giving is for the purpose of getting some kind of economic benefit (tax deduction, premium, public favor, better business, etc.).*

Biblical view: *Our giving is to God to acknowledge His ownership of everything; it is to be done out of the "firstfruits" not the leftovers (Proverbs 3:9).*

Beliefs about how ministry should be supported

Inaccurate belief: *Paul made tents for a living so people in full-time ministry should find ways to support themselves* **OR** *Fundraising is a secular invention, something Christian ministries should not engage in.*

Biblical view: *Jesus' ministry was supported by donors (Luke 8:1–3). Paul himself was supported by donors (Philippians 4:14–16) and wrote to the Corinthian church that ministry workers should be supported (1 Corinthians 9:14). In 2 Corinthians 8–9, Paul engages in a fundraising effort for the church in Jerusalem.*[2]

The following materials are adapted from Donna Wilson's workshop. Look for your own emotions and fears in the statements she offers, then dig into the Scriptures she's listed to provide a biblical response to each emotional barrier.[3]

Fear: lack of confidence

> *People question why I'm going into ministry.*
> *I could never feel confident about fundraising to do ministry.*
> *People will think all I care about is money.*
> *I am uncertain about my call. It isn't like my other colleagues in ministry.*

Scriptural truth: We do ministry in obedience to God's call in our lives (John 15:12–17, 1 Timothy 4:12–16, 2 Corinthians 4:1–15, 2 Timothy 1:3–14).

Scriptural truth: God calls us (1 Samuel 3:1–21, 1 Samuel 16:1–13, Isaiah 6:1–8, Jeremiah 1:1–10, Luke 5:1–11, Acts 9:1–18).

Feelings about money (which we tend to project onto donors)

> *Money is the root of all evil and contaminates Christian ministry.*
> *Money is a personal thing and shouldn't be talked about.*
> *Righteous living results in financial blessing.*
> *What I do with my money is my business.*
> *Poverty is more spiritual. Christians with money aren't living obediently.*
> *People won't give if they don't think I'm needy.*
> *Talking about money produces a lot of anxiety. Will there be enough?*

Scriptural truth: We are managers, not owners of the wealth God gives us and are called to be content and generous with money (Leviticus 25:23, 1 Chronicles 29:7–18, Psalm 24:1, Psalm 50:12, Deuteronomy 26:1–11, Haggai 2:6–9, Proverbs 3:9, 1 Timothy 6:6–19, Luke 12:13–34, Mark 10:17–31, Luke 16:10–13, Psalm 37:16).

Feeling: relational fear

> *Asking people to support my ministry feels wrong.*
> *Giving is personal. People should never be asked directly.*
> *Asking people for support will destroy my relationship with my friends.*

Scriptural truth: Paul boldly asks both for himself and others on the basis of a mutual commitment to the spread of the gospel and a bond of love (Philippians 1:1–21, 4:10–20, 2 Corinthians 8:1–9:15, Romans 15:18–24, 1 Corinthians 16:5–6, 2 Corinthians 1:15–16).

Fear: failure

> *Everyone is going to say no to my requests for support.*
> *I could go bankrupt if I have to rely on support.*
> *My donors determine my fate.*

Scriptural truth: God is our provider, not our donors (Deuteronomy 8; 1 Kings 17:8–16; Psalm 23; Psalm 37:25–29; Psalm 104; Isaiah 41:8–10; Matthew 6:19–33; Hebrews 6:10).

Feelings: shame, unworthiness

Fundraising is shameful. I feel like I'm begging. I should be able to support myself. I feel guilty asking for money. There are people needier than I am. Maybe I should just volunteer?

It feels wrong to be paid for doing something I love.

Scriptural truth: God commands appropriate compensation for Christian workers (1 Timothy 5:17–18; Deuteronomy 25:4; Luke 10:7; Matthew 10:10; Galatians 6:6; 1 Corinthians 9:14; 1 Samuel 21:3–6; 21–25; Isaiah 54:4).

Feeling: guilt

Fundraising is all about getting and not giving.

Raising support feels like a one-way relationship.

Isn't this just using people—building relationships to get money?

Scriptural truth: God created us for both giving and receiving and indicates those who give will reap spiritual rewards (Philippians 4:10–20; Matthew 10:5–13; 2 Corinthians 8:12–15; Deuteronomy 16:17; 2 Corinthians 9:7; Romans 12:1–12; Luke 6:38).

Fear: self-doubt

I don't have the gifts to do this.

I'm afraid I'm going to fail.

The need is so great, and I am so limited.

Scriptural truth: God has called us, and He will equip and empower us (1 Corinthians 1:25–31; 2 Corinthians 2:14–3:6; 1 Corinthians 12:4–24; 1 Timothy 4:14–16; 1 Peter 4:7–11; John 14:10–12).

Fear: nerves

When I think about fundraising, I am terrified.

I feel fearful whenever I'm making a call.

My hands shake when I'm making a presentation.

Scriptural truth: God is at work in and through us. He will accomplish his purposes (1 Peter 3:13–17; Exodus 4:1–17; Isaiah 50:4; Psalm 27; Psalm 145; Isaiah 43:1–7).

Feeling: discouragement

> *This job is too big; I'll never get fully funded.*
>
> *It seems as if I've been fundraising forever. I don't think I can keep going.*
>
> *I can't take the pressure; I need to give up.*

Scriptural truth: God calls us to let go of anxiety and remember with Him nothing is impossible (Psalm 55:22; Philippians 4:4–7; 1 Peter 5:6–7; Luke 1:37; Psalm 147; Luke 18:1–8; Matthew 6:25–34).

Feelings: selfishness, rejection

> *People don't want to give.*
>
> *Giving is only done out of obligation or guilt.*
>
> *When I get a no, it feels like personal rejection.*

Scriptural truth: God created humans to experience joy in giving and calls us not to take rejection personally (2 Corinthians 8:1–5; 2 Corinthians 9:6–15; Exodus 35:20–21; 36:2–7; 1 Chronicles 29:7–18; 2 Kings 4:8–22; 32–37; Matthew 10:40–42; Mark 6:7–10; 2 Chronicles 31:2–10).

Feeling: parental/family disapproval

> *My parents think ministry is nice but want to know when I'm going to get a "real" job.*
>
> *None of my family members are Christians, so what I'm doing doesn't make any sense to them.*
>
> *My parents are embarrassed that I'm asking people for money and have forbidden me to ask any of their friends.*
>
> *My family helped me through college; now I'm obligated to fulfill their expectations.*
>
> *I am the first one in my family/community to go to college. They feel I'm throwing away my education.*

Scriptural truth: We are called both to obey God and honor our parents (Exodus 20:12; Deuteronomy 5:16; Proverbs 3:11–12; Malachi 4:1–6; Matthew 10:34–39; Matthew 12:46–50; Matthew 19:27–29; Romans 12:9–13:3; Colossians 3:12–20, 1 Timothy 5:8).

Battling Discouragement

The truth from God's Word is always the best source for help and comfort, no matter what fears and feelings you battle as you tackle your fundraising objectives. What follows here is simply an overflow of encouragement in the form of "discouragement antidotes" from Betty Barnett of YWAM (Youth With A Mission).[4]

I call on the Lord in my distress, and he answers me. (Psalm 120:1)

I lift up my eyes to the hills—where does my help come from? My help comes from the Lord, the Maker of heaven and earth. He will not let your foot slip—he who watches over you will not slumber . . . he will watch over your life; the Lord will watch over your coming and going both now and forevermore. (Psalm 121:1–3, 7–8)

I sought the Lord, and he answered me; he delivered me from all my fears. Those who look to him are radiant; their faces are never covered with shame. . . . The angel of the Lord encamps around those who fear him, and he delivers them. (Psalm 34:4–5, 7)

Let us then approach the throne of grace with confidence, so that we may receive mercy and find grace to help us in our time of need . . . God is not unjust; he will not forget your work and the love you have shown him as you have helped his people and continue to help them . . . imitate those who through faith and patience inherit what has been promised. (Hebrews 4:16; 6:10, 12)

The Lord is faithful to all his promises and loving toward all he has made. (Psalm 145:13)

Therefore, my dear brothers, stand firm. Let nothing move you. Always give yourselves fully to the work of the Lord, because you know that your labor in the Lord is not in vain. (1 Corinthians 15:58)

The one who calls you is faithful and he will do it. (1 Thessalonians 5:24)

Now to him who is able to do immeasurably more than all we ask or imagine, according to his power that is at work within us. (Ephesians 3:20)

Summon your power, O God; show us your strength, O God, as you have done before. (Psalm 68:28)

I thank Christ Jesus our Lord, who has given me strength, that he considered me faithful, appointing me to his service. (1 Timothy 1:12)

Move Ahead with Confidence

We all have many stories on how fear can paralyze. We dare not let fear distract us from accomplishing God's purpose for our lives. Move forward with full confidence that the Lord has called you and will meet your every need for His purposes.

Confidence comes from experience.

Many of you experience not only fear but lack of confidence. I have good news for you: Confidence comes from experience. The more calls you make, the more visits you make, the more you will begin to see your confidence pick up.

CHAPTER 5

It's Really Not About You

I am convinced that God is in the business of translating His agenda into the hearts of His people. If you are truly called to ministry you have been given an assignment and a vision to accomplish. Now you have the unique opportunity and privilege to give God's people an opportunity to be a financial part of His program.

When you get down to it, you are not asking for yourself but asking for funds to allow you to accomplish God's vision through you.

A key perspective is that you are giving God's people an opportunity to invest and partner in God's eternal program. Remember, it is more blessed to give. This really takes the focus away from you and puts it back on giving people the opportunity to partner. I firmly believe your donors have a greater need to give than you have to receive. Let me put it this way: Your donors might need you more than you need them. Think about that.

There is no need to beg or pressure. You are merely sharing your vision and helping to bring people to a decision. While we are on the subject of vision, remember that the vision is the place to keep your focus. It would be easy to assemble a list of your needs—the need for a salary, medical benefits, retirement, car fund, and so many other things. If you were to present your list of needs, that surely would not excite me. I, like other donors, want to know what my money will do to further the gospel. Spell out that vision loud and clear. Scott Morton, with the Navigators, says, "We must remember we are inviting supporters to advance the kingdom, not merely to meet our personal needs."[1] You are merely an agent called of God to engage His people in

His program—not your program, your needs, your budget.

It's not really about you, but our culture strongly emphasizes personal autonomy. Our culture promotes independence; God promotes dependence–on Him and His church. Because of your immersion in our culture, you may feel quite uncomfortable by receiving gifts from others. Yet the Lord has designed each part of the body of Christ to function in interdependence with other parts of the body.

> *Your donors have a greater need to give than you have to receive.*

God's Design and Purposes for Your Prospects and Donors

Since it's not really about you, let's focus for a bit on your prospects and donors and what the Lord may have in His plans for them. If they are believers, they are stewards—and not owners—of what God has given.

Randy Alcorn describes the Christian's ideal position on finances through six keys given in his book *The Treasure Principle.*

Key 1: God owns everything. I'm His money manager. (We are the managers of the assets God has entrusted—not given—to us.)

Key 2: My heart always goes where I put God's money. (Watch what happens when you reallocate your money from temporal things to eternal things.)

Key 3: Heaven, not earth, is my home. (We are citizens of "a better country—a heavenly one." Hebrews 11:16)

Key 4: I should live not for the dot but for the line. (From the dot—our present life on earth—extends a line that goes on forever, which is eternity in heaven.)

Key 5: Giving is the only antidote to materialism. (Giving is the joyful surrender to a greater Person and a greater agenda. It dethrones me and exalts Him.)

Key 6: God prospers me not to raise my standard of living but to raise my standard of giving. (God gives us more money than we need so we can give—generously.)[2]

In his book *The Genius of Generosity,* Chip Ingram identifies six areas over which God's people are stewards, while God is the owner. Many Christians have never considered God's ownership of so much of their lives!

1. ***Our time.*** Psalm 75:2 tells us that our time is not actually ours but is entrusted to us.
2. ***Our spouses.*** Proverbs 19:14 reminds us that our spouses come from the Lord.
3. ***Our property.*** Luke 16:12 says that we're to be trustworthy with the property given to us.
4. ***Our spiritual gifts.*** Romans 12:6 indicates that we receive spiritual gifts by God's grace.
5. ***God's truth.*** First Corinthians 4:1 calls us servants who have been "entrusted with [truth,] the secret things of God."
6. ***Our bodies.*** Even our bodies, according to 1 Corinthians 6:19–20, don't belong to us. We are bought with a price.[3]

Your Role as Fundraiser

As a fundraiser you play a critical role in the balance between God (the owner) and other believers (the stewards). You might see your role in several ways.

Transfer Agent or Facilitator

You have the interesting role of becoming the eyes and ears, hands and feet for your donors. Chip Ingram tells how he met with a Christian businessman in Dallas, who made three observations:

"Number one, I would desire to help poor and hurting people.

"Number two, you are in contact with poor and hurting people daily.

"Number three, I want you to be my eyes and ears and help them as God leads you."

Then the businessman handed Chip a check for $5,000. Chip responded, "Do you mean you want me to figure out who to help and then help them the way you would if you saw the situation?"

The man responded, "That's exactly what I want you to do, Chip."[4]

As you raise funds for your ministry, you're investing your donors' money and your time to accomplish God's purposes. Remember, it's really not about you.

The Motivator

Your passion and vision can inspire people to give. But keep in mind your job description does not include putting prospects on a guilt trip. No, it's a journey that you take them on that should result in a cheerful heart giving back to the Lord. Scripture tells us that "God loves a cheerful giver" (2 Corinthians 9:7). "Giving is meant to be joyful and fulfilling," Ingram notes. "It isn't rooted in guilt, self-righteousness, or a martyr complex. It's rooted in joy."[5]

Sharer of the Privilege

As you introduce your prospects to your work, you offer them the privilege to engage in the greatest program on earth. There is none better! Notice how Ingram refers to stewardship: "Biblical stewardship is a truly beautiful thing. Why? Because it's an amazing privilege that God has given especially to us."[6]

Did you catch that? Privilege. Now let's apply that to your situation. You're going to ask people for funds for your ministry. I have so often heard people say, "I just hate to obligate people," but that's wrong in the biblical sense. You are offering people the privilege of partnering with you in the Lord. If you, your family, or friends consider your ministry "begging," then you certainly don't have God's perspective on this. "True generosity flows out of an understanding that God owns everything. In His economy, good stewardship is by nature generous and joyful; it directs his resources extravagantly toward his purposes and for his people to deeply enjoy. If we want to understand generosity biblically, we need to see stewardship through new lenses—less as a reluctant obligation and more as a golden opportunity."[7]

The Cheerleader

As your donors give and God blesses, you have the wonderful opportunity to share what God is doing, thank them, and engage them in an interactive relationship with you and your work. You will have some happy donors praising God for His faithfulness.

Stewardship Partner

As your donors exercise stewardship by giving to your ministry, you share in their stewardship by becoming a steward of their monies. Both of you are respecting God as the owner as you work in tandem.

Because fundraising is not really about you, I'd pose three questions you might ask yourself on a consistent basis. These are the questions Chip Ingram says that smart stewards ask themselves:

1. Am I using the money entrusted to me in accordance with the owner's wishes?

2. Am I carefully keeping an account of where the owner's funds are going?

3. Am I becoming best friends with the owner by managing his resources?[7]

As founder and director of Inner City Impact, I take very seriously the responsibility I have of being a good steward of the funds given to me to manage. I hope that's true of you as well.

The Tutor

As you undertake People Raising, you'll find people's experience of giving falls all across the continuum from folks who have never given to those who give consistently out of a heart of generosity. In some cases you may very well become a sort of tutor for your donors. Some of your contacts will be people who are just beginning to learn about giving. The Lord can use you to introduce them to the principles of stewardship. What a blessing for both you and your donor, as your faith grows as you watch God work. "Faith increases giving, and giving increases faith."[8]

What you and I are promoting is a lifestyle. People Raising is a journey on your part, but never forget that your donors are on a similar journey. As both of you play your roles, God's work will be advanced and He will be glorified.

CHAPTER 6

The Number One Enemy of Fundraising

D.L. Moody once said, "I've never met a man who has given me as much trouble as myself."

This is oh-so-true when it comes to raising funds. Negative thinking can lead you down a road of no return.

1. Negative thinking produces negative *thoughts*.
2. Negative thoughts produce negative *actions*.
3. Negative actions produce negative *results*.

Negative Thinking Influences Your Prospect List

This progression of negativity most impacts fundraising in the area of how we build our lists and choose prospective donors. Negative thinking tells me I should not put on my list a person who already gives to numerous individuals and organizations. Negative thinking tells me not to bother with those who are strapped with financial obligations—for example, sending kids through college.

In other words, *my* negative thinking stands in the way of another person's freedom to make a decision. Don't let negative thinking eliminate prospective donors. Build your list positively, and allow your contacts to make their own decision whether to give to you or your organization. Don't make that decision for them.

Negative Thinking Keeps You from Challenging People

Negative thinking can get in the way of our challenge to others. Negative thinking tells me I should ask for a minimal gift, lowballing the asking amount.

Here's an example; you might notice that prospective donors recently purchased a new home and conclude that the family must be strapped for money. So you take the decision out of their hands by asking for a small gift.

> *The decision to give is not yours; let your prospects make the decision.*

Again, this negative thinking closes a door of opportunity—or at least narrows how wide it may open. My advice is to go ahead and challenge people high. Let your donors make the decision, not you.

Negative Thinking Impairs Follow-Up

Negative thinking badly hampers the important step of your follow-up of a person you have asked for a gift but who wants time to consider your request.

Negative thoughts can keep you from placing that call. With a bit of imagination, you can think up a dozen reasons why *not* to place that follow-up call.

The Enemy of Deputation Was Me

If you find yourself getting in your own way in fundraising, take heart. You're in good company, and not just with D. L. Moody. Curtis Kregness of the ministry New Life Editions underscores this issue in his article "The 'Enemy' of Deputation Was Me."

I entered deputation with some apprehension, not really knowing what to expect, but realizing that I was in for a long, arduous climb. I was convinced of one thing—that God was going to have to take up the slack in many places, because I felt very inadequate for a public relations-type ministry, especially when it often centered on myself. . . .

But as I climbed further up the mountain, I discovered that someone had not told me the complete story. God was using the deputation experience to minister to me. At each new bend in the trail, I realized some new lesson that God was teaching me, which went far beyond the fundraising and prayer-raising function of deputation. . . .

The comic strip character named Pogo once uttered this piece of wisdom: "We have met the enemy and he is us!" My deputation experience verified that often we are our own worst enemies.[1]

I'll never forget visiting a friend of our family. He operated a construction business. I walked into his construction yard and headed toward his small, concrete-block office. Before I got to the door, I heard my name called out. Initially I didn't know where the voice was coming from. Then I looked high in the sky, and there on top of a piece of construction equipment was our friend. He was an interesting, colorful character. You never knew exactly what he would say next. He yelled from the top of the construction equipment, "Bill, have you heard? The devil is going out of business! He's selling all his equipment, but he's saving one thing: the tool of discouragement."

That visit occurred many years ago, but I still replay it in my mind. For each of us, discouragement is very present and it impacts our fundraising. It is just another example of negative thinking.

I face negative thinking constantly in my role as a fundraiser. I begin to list all the reasons why I should not pursue a prospect. As I list these reasons, I try to convince myself. On many occasions, thank the Lord, I recognize that I need to let the prospects make the decision, not me. That's all negative thinking.

Once I've crossed that threshold of pursuing a prospect, then it's my nervousness about placing the phone call. There are times when I close my office door, so that my staff can't sense my nervousness and fear. Before picking up the phone to place a call asking for an appointment, I take one last, quick breath, calm my nerves, pray to the Lord, and dial the number. The phone rings once, then twice, a third time, and fourth time. I breathe a sigh of relief: Good. No one is home. Though I go through this exercise on a regular basis, I've learned that it's worth it.

There is not a month that goes by when I don't think back about a contact with a major prospect. Negative thinking was closing in on me. I was sure he would not take my call. If he did, would he give me an appointment? Even if he gave me the appointment, would he really be sincerely interested in my ministry? I doubted he would even give that much. He already gave to many major ministries. Why would he even consider my ministry? If I were to share this man's name and his position, you would understand why all these questions and negative thinking were at the forefront of my mind. But I refused to be defeated by negative thinking. I placed the call, got the appointment, asked for the biggest amount I had ever asked for. He asked for time to pray and consider. He came back and offered double the amount I had asked for.

Later, this donor visited Inner City Impact, and he was thrilled to see how his funds had been used. He gave another, similar gift several months later. I continue to talk with him, and yet I must admit that negative thinking and nervousness and fear are *still* with me. The fear certainly has been reduced, but it has not been eliminated. Recently I took the opportunity to call and give him an update. Without any prompting on my part, he said, "I know that when I'm face to face with the Lord, I'll never be embarrassed about my giving to you and your ministry." Through that scenario, I had battled negative thinking, but the Lord gave me victory. As you can sense, it was worth it all.

Raising funds is ministry.

Like you, I experience negative thinking. You and I are the number one enemies of fundraising. When it comes to negative thinking, there are two outcomes. In the first, we give in to the negative thinking, and the process of raising funds is dragged out unnecessarily. Instead of engaging in the ministry the Lord has called us to, we end up treading water. The second outcome is that we recognize negative thinking for what it is. With the Lord's help, we face it and let the Lord and the prospect make the decision about who will participate in the ministry and vision the Lord has given us.

Who is the number one enemy of fundraising? It is *you* and *me*. We need encouragement from God's Word to "be strong and courageous" (Joshua 1:9). In many cases we need an attitude change. Take the time to biblically correct your own attitudes and beliefs about ministry and money, God's work and God's resources.

This is crucial. Each of us needs to proceed with a positive attitude and vision for the assignments God has given us. Remember, raising funds is ministry. The Lord is expanding your ministry to include people who will pray for and support your cause.

Raising funds is ministry.

Cultivating the
NECESSARY SKILLS
for
RAISING FUNDS

CHAPTER 7

Develop a Fundraising Strategy

Anyone new to fundraising will discover a host of ideas out there on how to go about raising funds. What's the best way to sift out the best advice? Unfortunately, a lot of advice comes from those who have actually never raised funds. Those who have experience with fundraising recognize the need for a structured plan.

If you are raising funds, you must develop a strategy. A plan starts with the conviction that God already has chosen those people to support you or your ministry. As you follow His direction, He will lead you to people who are willing and able to give.

Two Key Principles

In my many years of fundraising I have identified two key principles.

Principle 1: Relationships

People give to people.
People give to people they know.
People give to people they know and trust.
People give to people they know, trust, and care for.

This principle can be summed up in one word: *relationships*. Because fundraising is developing relationships among caring people, start by contacting people the Lord has already brought across your path—people who know you, trust you, and care about you. A common mistake made by those seeking to raise funds is to go to people with whom they have no relationship. They assume that just because they are Christians called to ministry that other Christians will naturally want to support them.

In later chapters you will learn how to broaden your contacts by meeting new people in a logical and natural way.

Principle 2: Personal and Practical

The key to raising funds successfully is to personally contact people you know in the most personal and practical way possible.

What does that mean? The *Harvard Business Review* studied the forms of communication and ranked them according to effectiveness in the following order. Since the time of their study, new forms of communication have been created such as e-mail, Facebook, and other social media, but take a look at the chart on the right to see what comes to the surface.

The most effective form of communication is one-on-one, and fundraising forms diminish in effectiveness the more impersonal they become. So your fundraising plan should be relational, as well as personal and practical.

As you form your plan, evaluate the advice and systems you encounter against those two principles. To what extent are they employing the most effective methods of communicating their message?

Most fundraising systems have two major problems—and both violate our two principles. The first problem is what I call "the shotgun approach." Eager to raise support, the fundraiser rushes off

1.	One-on-one
2.	Small group discussion
3.	Large group discussion
4.	Telephone
5.	Handwritten letter
6.	Typed letter
7.	Mass letter
8.	Newsletter
9.	Brochure
10.	News item
11.	Advertisement
12.	Handout

in every direction. He or she looks through the yellow pages for any church that might have an evangelical tag. Unfortunately they wander into the unknown and waste time, energy, and money contacting people who don't know them, trust them, or have a deep concern for them. That violates principle 1.

The second problem is a strategy of fundraising using impersonal tools. Time and finances are spent on mass mailings to long lists of people. When letters don't produce the desired results, fundraisers get discouraged, give up, and never see their ministry or organization fully funded.

> *The most effective form of communication is one-on-one.*

Letter writing has its place, but notice that place according to the *Harvard Business Review* survey: Mail is ranked the fifth, sixth, and seventh best methods for effective communicating. Letters alone will not get the job done. The primary focus for communicating your vision must be one-on-one visits.

One-on-one is important because communicating is not just about words. Only 7 percent of communication is done through words. Ninety-three percent comes through expression, gestures, tone, and body language. A personal, face-to-face meeting provides vital two-way communication.

Two Case Studies: Jonathan and Julie

Let me describe to you two actual cases of individuals who tried to raise funds. Jonathan's approach was less effective than Julie's, though his heart, no doubt, was in the right place. Jonathan's focus was on impersonal tools.

Miles driven: 33,000
Money spent on direct expenses (not personal): $8,530
Monthly financial support needed: $2,000

• Churches contacted	164
• Information packs sent	155
• Pastoral meetings set up after sending information packs	58
• Meetings resulting from the 58 pastoral meetings	26 with 9 pledging support
• Meetings from phone calls after sending packs	8 with 2 pledging support

▪ Meetings from churches of family	6 with 5 pledging support
▪ Meetings from churches calling me	3 with 0 pledging support
▪ Churches spoken in	43
▪ Churches spoken in twice	4
▪ Churches spoken in many times	4
▪ Bible study	1
▪ Total meetings	51+

This man interacted with forty-three churches, but only sixteen provided financial support. Those sixteen churches represent 75 percent of the monthly support. The remaining 25 percent is made up of individuals.

Note the strong focus on church meetings, rather than meetings with individuals. Also note the miles driven and the cost—and consider how long it is taking to get the needed funds.

Julie forms a positive contrast. Julie focused her fundraising efforts on individuals. She raised her full support in ten weeks through the following process.

- Sent an initial letter to 106 of her friends.
- Called forty-one of those people seeking an appointment.
- Thirty-eight agreed to meet with her.
- Thirty-one agreed to support her.

Another person agreed to support Julie later. Another person's company gave a substantial gift. Another group promised a gift, and she met with four people who did not give; she will pursue them when additional funds are necessary. In addition to those thirty-eight appointments, Julie saw the Lord bring in additional gifts when four people who did not even receive a letter heard about her through the grapevine or met her for the first time and decided to support her. Five people who only received a letter (and no follow-up phone call) responded in a positive way to support her. Three people who received letters and follow-up calls, but had no appointments, agreed to support her. Finally, she received a call from someone who had only heard of her, and that person agreed to support her as well.

Note the brief time (ten weeks), the focus on individuals, the good response she had in setting up appointments (thirty-eight out of forty-one), and how God worked above her strategy to bring in additional gifts.

I believe in high tech (using all communication forms available) and high touch (ongoing personal interaction) when it comes to raising funds. Visiting with prospective donors is cost-effective and time-effective and can result in a highly committed team of supporters.

Where Do You Go from Here?

When you start to raise funds, apply the first principle. Systematically identify whom you will target—people who already know, trust, and care about you. Those individuals become your audience and the foundation on which you will build your fundraising strategy. Then apply principle 2, systematically meeting one-on-one with as many as is possible and practical. By doing so, you will:

- Renew and strengthen friendships.
- Make new friends.
- Experience God working in and through you.
- Develop ministry and communication skills.
- Offer people an opportunity to partner with you through their financial gifts and prayers.

The people you contact will benefit. These friends who know, trust, and care about you will:

- Experience God's blessing as they give financially.
- Gain a new perspective on how God is working.

Even back in 90 A.D., the apostle John seemed to understand the importance of meeting with people face-to-face. He wrote, "I have much to write to you, but I do not want to use paper and ink. Instead, I hope to visit you and talk with you face to face, so that our joy may be complete" (2 John 1:12).

If I could give you only one word of advice, it would be to see people personally. There is no question about it: The strategy of going to people personally will work for you as you follow these twelve steps:

Step 1: Begin with your home church.

Step 2: Determine to whom you will go for funds.

Step 3: Record, catalog, and prioritize your prospects.

Step 4: Get the word out.

Step 5: Make appointments.

Step 6: Conduct the visit.

Step 7: Track funds.

Step 8: Say thank you.

Step 9: Conduct a phone appointment .

Step 10: Expand your contacts .

Step 11: Cultivate your donors.

Step 12: Resolicit funds.

The remainder of this section will look at each of these twelve steps, one by one.

CHAPTER 8

STEP 1:
Begin with Your Home Church

D o you have a home church? Because of college, a job move, a sense of hesitation to "lock in" to one church, or a few other reasons, some who sense God's call are not affiliated with one church. If that is your situation, you need to understand the importance of being part of a local church and you should begin to develop a relationship with a church.

Sometimes fundraisers encounter a problem because they do not have a "home church." I don't want you to skip step 1, but if you don't have a home church at present, you can begin with step 2—with the understanding that you will return to this chapter soon.

As you think of your home church, always start with the pastor. In some cases he is the decision maker when it comes to providing financial support. If he is not, it could be a missions pastor or a missions committee. You need to find who that decision maker is.

In 1972 when I began Inner City Impact, I was eager to share the gospel with the children of Humboldt Park in Chicago's inner city. But I didn't know who would provide the funds. As my wife, Sandy, and I looked forward to starting a family, we wondered, *Where will the funds come from?*

We didn't join an established organization but had to venture out by faith. But we were confident that God would supply. The Holy Spirit prodded us: "This is the way; walk in it." So seeking spiritual direction, I began by calling my pastor.

Contacting the Pastor

It is a great thrill for a pastor to know that a member of his congregation is obeying God's call to Christian service. So set a time to meet with your senior pastor or whoever is the decision maker on providing financial support, and share your burden for the ministry the Lord has called you to.

My pastor was a visionary—a man who spoke quickly, listened intently, and offered timely advice. As I think back, I'm sure I saw the glimmer in his eye as he began to catch my burden for the inner city. I know he saw the glimmer in mine.

Understanding my tremendous financial needs, he promised to help. He suggested ways I might share my vision with the church, and eventually the church decided to carry part of our support. In addition, many individuals from my home church contributed money, time, and energy to our ministry.

By contacting your pastor first, you recognize him as a spiritual leader and seek his approval before proceeding to enlist support from your church. You will benefit from his counsel now and in the days ahead. You need to have him on your team.

You need to have your pastor on your team.

Because the pastor is a key decision maker, he can recommend you, for example, to the missions committee and to potential supporters both inside and outside your church. He can explain the process for securing financial support and suggest ways you might minister in the church. His approval—or disapproval—of your plans for Christian service will help determine how much financial support the church will give. So begin to build a working relationship with your pastor.

Because church organizational structures are different, be flexible. In large churches, it may be impossible to meet with the senior pastor. Instead, you will be referred to an associate staff person. He may have the authority to recommend you to the missions committee and to others. Once you have met with the associate minister or committee leader, the door may be opened to meeting with the senior pastor later.

Be sensitive to your pastor's schedule and workload. I never call pastors on Mondays because many pastors take Mondays off. And I don't call on Wednesdays because they are often preparing for the midweek service. I never call Fridays because many pastors are preparing for their Sunday sermons. By calling on a Tuesday or Thursday, I am most likely to get ahold of the pastor and be able to set a time to meet.

Goals for Meeting with a Pastor

What you accomplish in your meeting with a pastor depends on how thoroughly you prepare. I can think of five goals for your meeting.

Articulate Your Vision

Your first goal is to articulate how God led you into Christian ministry and your burden and vision. I suggest that you write out your vision and rehearse it. Stand in front of a mirror, or sit in a comfortable chair, and practice your presentation. Talk enthusiastically and with conviction about what God has called you to do.

Gather literature on your organization, including a doctrinal statement and supporting materials. Bring them when you meet. If your pastor is not familiar with your organization, such printed pieces will explain the organization's operation and give him confidence. If time permits, and a DVD or a website is available, watch a presentation or check out the website together.

Share the Financial Need

Your second goal is to share your financial need. When asked how much financial support you must raise, don't sidestep the issue. Be straightforward and state the financial goal. Indicate what that includes—for example, outgoing or start-up expenses, transportation, and shipping of personal goods, insurance, housing, equipment, and other needs. Be prepared to answer questions such as, "How much financial support do you have pledged currently? What is your target date to leave for your assignment/begin your ministry? What will be your specific assignment?"

Find Out How to Make a Formal Request for Support

Discussing your vision and need is not enough. Your third goal is to gain a clear understanding regarding what steps you should follow to make a formal request for financial support from your specific home church.

You will need to ask these essential questions:

1. Does the church have particular policies or procedures for requesting support?
2. Who makes the decision? Is it the pastor, the missions committee, or church board?

3. Who is the chairperson of that committee or board? What is his/her phone number? What is the person's e-mail address?
4. How often does the committee meet? When is the next meeting?
5. Who are the members of that committee?
6. What qualifications are set by the committee for those seeking financial support?
7. What are the steps for making application? Is there an application form to be completed?
8. Does the committee designate a set amount for a single person, a married couple, a married couple with children? If so, what is that amount?
9. Are there any deadlines? For example, when does the committee set the budget for the next year?

Identify Ways to Present Your Ministry

Because one church rarely provides the total support for a single ministry, you will also need to enlist individual supporters within the church. For that to happen people need to meet you and catch your vision.

Your fourth goal is to identify ways to present your ministry to the church. Because the key person to opening doors of opportunity in the church is often the senior pastor, ask him for ideas on where you might minister in the church. Discuss options such as:

- Sunday morning worship service—giving a three- to five-minute presentation or, if you are qualified, preaching
- Sunday school teaching or presentation
- Youth activities
- Midweek service/prayer meeting
- Missions committee meeting—making a presentation
- Retreat, conference, camp—giving a presentation
- Vacation Bible School
- Small groups/Bible studies

My pastor called me late one Monday evening. He explained he had a bad case of food poisoning and asked if I would teach the women's Bible study the next morning. I was happy for the opportunity and got up early Tuesday morning to prepare. As I spoke, I added illustrations from our ICI ministry.

Several days later I received a check for $500 for ICI from one woman who had been in the Bible study. Today gifts from those women continue to come. They first caught the vision for our ministry at that Bible study, and they have increased their support through the years.

You must be willing—sometimes—to teach a class, help in the nursery or with the youth, or to be involved in other ways. Help in any capacity you can, but don't tie yourself down as you need to have flexibility to schedule other fundraising meetings.

Ask the Pastor for Introductions

Your fifth goal is to ask the pastor to introduce you to other contacts—both inside and outside your church. When a dear Christian woman became a widow, she wanted to give some of her money to ministries. She asked her pastor for advice, and he recommended she include Inner City Impact in her giving.

After receiving the first gift, I phoned to thank her and began to develop a friendship with her. Today she is deeply committed to our ministry and gives liberally every year. She also has included ICI in her will.

When you talk with your pastor, be prepared to take notes. List potential ministry opportunities and people to contact.

Contacts You May Develop through Your Pastor

Your pastor may put you in contact with:

- Christian businesspeople
- Another pastor who would permit you to share your ministry in his church
- A local ministerial association through which you can meet area pastors
- Various Bible study groups
- Members of your congregation who share an enthusiasm for your type of ministry or who give generously to kingdom work

I continue to maintain contact with pastors of our supporting churches and invite them and their wives to special ICI events. In addition, I encourage them to bring businesspeople from their churches with them as guests.

Our supporters include six businessmen who became regular support- ers. I initially met each of them because I asked a pastor to introduce me to key professionals who might be able to support our ministry. As God blesses these men, they often look for additional ways to give back to the Lord.

Your Ministry to the Pastor

Your meeting with your pastor will give you opportunity to minister to him as well. Your willingness to be available and involved in the church will encourage him. As you talk together, show genuine interest in his ministry and family; his goals for the church; ministry areas he enjoys; his problems, frustrations, and concerns; ways that he would like to see the church grow; and ways people are responding in the church. Affirm your pastor and empathize with him.

Yet remember the purpose for your visit. Your focus is on seeing your financial support need met. So before you leave, ask him to recommend the next step for you to take in raising financial support.

You Are a Member of a Family

Whatever the ministry God has called you to, you are not alone. You are a member of a church family. As you raise financial support, it will be church family members who pray for you, rejoice with you, encourage you through the discouraging times, and contribute financially. That kind of support comes when you have made the effort to be interested and involved in the church and its members.

In the early days of our ministry, we eagerly checked the mail each day for any envelope that might contain a financial gift. When gifts came, many were small. But they added up, and we thanked God for providing for our needs. When one couple from a former church sent a gift of several hundred dollars, we were elated. That gift made a significant difference to us and was a sign that somebody understood the ministry we were launching.

That first meeting with my pastor was nearly forty years ago. Our family has grown to include three children. The Inner City Impact ministry that began with children on a sidewalk now ministers in three needy communities in the Chicago area.

We've used the principles in this book to help our staff raise financial support for those communities. As the work continues to expand and the financial needs increase, God's provisions have been miraculous. But His provision doesn't come automatically. It is a result of developing relationships with people God has led us to contact.

Be Flexible

Because each church organizational structure is different, the suggestions in this chapter are just that—suggestions. Adjust them depending on your situation and your specific church family.

Do not be discouraged if you don't come away from the initial meeting with your pastor with a list of confirmed speaking engagements. Churches have limited speaking opportunities, and pastors have many requests. Be willing to take advantage of any opportunity your pastor offers. Thank the Lord for openings even if you cannot see how a specific engagement will help you raise financial support.

God will direct your ministry and provide in surprising ways in the days ahead. The key is to take specific notes when you meet with your pastor and follow up on the suggestions he makes.

God will direct and provide in surprising ways in the days ahead.

Securing financial support from the church is key, but your job is not done. Take the opportunity to contact individuals within the church who can lend their financial support as well.

Because it is unlikely your home church will take on your full support, meeting with your pastor is just the first of twelve steps to take in raising financial support. Before proceeding with this step of meeting with the pastor, continue reading until you grasp all twelve steps and fully understand our fundraising philosophy and strategy.

CHAPTER 9

STEP 2:
Determine to Whom You Will Go for Funds

Looking for prospective supporters is an ongoing process, not a one-time function. In fact, you will never finish building your list of prospects; you will always be on the lookout for new prospects.

Compile a Prospect List

You will be surprised by how quickly a prospect list grows when you think of people by categories.

If you are married, you and your spouse should compile separate lists and then combine your contacts. As you build your list, remember negative thinking can cause you to eliminate people. Be inclusive, ready to let people make the decision whether they will support you.

Social Media Contacts

Welcome to the world of social media. Today we are most familiar with Facebook, Twitter, and others, but who knows what new social technologies will be rolled out in years to come. Whatever the application might be called, it will still be another way of capturing names you can add to your database. This alone should give you a great starting point. Don't be so concerned about how small or large your list might be.

Facebook is a great way to connect with old friends as well as make new friends. But you won't want to jump right into these new connections with old and new friends by suddenly talking about money. Take the opportunity to reconnect and rebuild the relationship. At some point, you will be able to comfortably share your vision and ask these friends to be part of your support team.

Church Contacts

Begin with contacts in *the church you currently attend.* Go through your church directory name by name. Add to your list the names of people with whom you and your family have had contact. Do not merely put the entire church directory on your list. Consider people you have met through special groups such as church committees, Sunday school, Bible studies, care groups, boards, and so on. Add the names of camp friends and contacts from church conferences.

Move on to contacts from *churches you've attended in the past.* Think of past church staff—pastors, youth pastors, and office support staff. Remember the people you had contact with in the past in Sunday school classes and committee work. Cast your mind back to include churches you attended while at college and during summers.

As I built my list of church contacts, I thought about a church I had attended in my grade school days. I remembered Sherrill, who had married a doctor and now lived in Arizona. When I contacted her, she decided to support our ministry regularly. To this day she continues to lend her support.

Another couple I knew from my junior high years agreed to take on financial support when I contacted them.

As you work with these church contacts, remember the ideal: church support, plus support from individuals.

Relatives

Not only can relatives lend their financial support, they can catch the vision of the ministry as well. I represent the third generation of my family to serve Chicago's inner city since 1918.

As my wife, Sandy, was going through a list of her relatives, she thought of her cousin Jim, who lived in the Indianapolis area. When Jim was in Chicago, we invited him to tour our facilities and later challenged him to give. He has been supporting the ministry monthly ever since.

On your prospect list, include your parents, brothers, sisters, grandparents, children, aunts/uncles, cousins, nieces/nephews, and other relatives. Before you finish this category, talk to other family members. When I spoke with my dad, I learned that one of his cousins, a man I had never met, had accumulated some wealth. I made several phone calls and a visit, and eventually his family foundation decided to give an annual gift.

Neighbors

Neighbors can be a source of support. One of our neighbors heard me on a radio interview. Later he saw newspaper articles on our ministry and became a donor.

School Contacts

Review yearbooks, school directories, and class pictures. Social media again can be a tool to identify and locate former classmates. Your college alumni office and its publications and lists can be still another resource. Think about contacts you had through sports, clubs, Bible studies, and other school activities in: grade school, junior high, high school, college, and graduate school.

Don't forget special teachers, administrators, coaches, and other staff. Also list contacts from special Christian groups—for example, Youth for Christ, Young Life, Fellowship of Christian Athletes, Navigators, Campus Crusade for Christ, InterVarsity, etc.

Keep in mind that one goal of Christian professors is to see students become involved in full-time ministry. Add them to your prospect list.

Employment

Turn your attention to your work history. Add to your prospective donor list the supervisors, owners, fellow workers, customers, clients, vendors, professional acquaintances, salespeople, and anyone else you had contact with during your employment. Consider contacting your parents' employers, too. Think about past jobs (full- and part-time) as well as your current job.

During my junior high and high school days I mowed lawns, did yard work, and shoveled snow. Little did I realize that those relationships from so many years ago would produce donors to a ministry one day.

Service Contacts

Consider the following list of professional and service contacts:

- Barber or beautician
- Dry cleaners

- Dentist/orthodontist
- Doctors (family doctor, pediatrician, surgeon, specialists, eye doctor, and so on)
- Accountants
- Insurance agents (home, health, car, business)
- Lawyers
- Brokers
- Bankers
- Mechanics
- Plumbers
- Babysitters/preschool teachers
- Home sales contacts (Avon, Pampered Chef, Tupperware, etc.)
- Printers
- Christian bookstore owners
- Contractors
- Others

You may even want to check your chamber of commerce directory. It might jog your memory with other names of local business owners you've encountered.

Friends

You probably have more friends and acquaintances than you even realize. As you build your list of prospective supporters:

- Review your Facebook list.
- Review your Christmas list.
- Review your parents' Christmas list.
- If married, review your wedding guest book.
- Review your address book.
- Pull up your cell phone contact history.
- Review your family address book.
- Check your e-mail's digital address book.
- Remember people with whom you have shared hobbies, sports, and other interests.

My wife and I attended Murray State University in western Kentucky. At school, I led several Bible studies. One study met in the home of a dear couple. That couple was on the guest list for our wedding, and eventually we added them to our prospect list. How exciting it has been to see them catch a vision for our ministry and begin to support us.

Contacts from Your Ministry

Don't write off other Christian workers in your own ministry too quickly. Often I have seen board members and Christian workers lend their support. That could also include administrators and personnel department staff. I think of one missionary couple who made an impression on one of our board members. The couple received not only financial support but gifts each Christmas.

Friends from Other Ministry Organizations

It may seem to defy logic, but those involved in ministry make great givers. You might be tempted to leave Christian workers off your list, thinking they have many financial needs of their own and wouldn't be able to support your ministry. Remember the rule about letting the potential donor make the decision. You may be surprised how many people really enjoy giving.

Club and Civic Group Contacts

Don't forget contacts from such civic groups as Rotary, Kiwanis, Lions, Optimist, and others. Consider school contacts through the local parent-teacher organizations (PTO/PTA). You may have met people through neighborhood prayer groups or neighborhood watch associations, or you may be involved in a Christian Business Association.

Do you have military contacts or belong to professional associations or unions? These may be sources for your prospective donor list.

Corporations and Foundations

For most people raising funds, corporations and foundations are not really a viable option, though it can work if you've had some natural connection with them. In other words, it can work if you have personal access to a decision maker. I'll offer a word of caution: Attempting to enlist support from random corporations produces little. Therefore, be highly selective of foundations that you choose to approach. Identify someone with whom you have a relationship to be your advocate in approaching the decision makers.

As I added the name of a particular Christian foundation to my list, I admitted I knew very little about them. But one day while speaking at a Bible college, I was offered a tour of the campus and noticed a plaque on a building. Reading the inscription, I discovered that the foundation on my list was responsible for the funding of that building.

God already has all the people necessary to provide your full financial support.

The tour guide gave me the name of a key person who could introduce me to the foundation. I followed through, and our organization now receives an annual gift from that foundation.

Think Inclusively

As you develop your prospect list, pray for the people on it. Ask the Lord to bring to mind the names of those you need to contact. Pray for the people on your prospect list.

Do not write people off, assuming they can't possibly help, perhaps because you know they are already giving to six other Christian organizations or they have three kids in college.

Several years ago an Inner City Impact worker suggested that one of the donors who was supporting him personally might also give to our organization. The donor was a successful Christian businessman. My first thought was that he was overcommitted and would not consider helping our ministry. But fortunately I didn't listen to my own initial negative thinking. I eventually set up an appointment. Over the years, that man has provided major gifts for our ministry. I am so happy I did not let negative thinking set in.

Remember that God already has all the people necessary to provide your full financial support. Wait on the Lord, and ask the Holy Spirit for wisdom to challenge potential donors.

After you have completed your list, invite a friend or relative to review it. Ask if he or she can think of other names to add.

The List That Never Ends

You will never finish your list of prospects. You will always need to stay on the lookout for new contacts. Take up every opportunity you can to get your message out and meet new people. I have a saying that is oh-so-true: Visibility equals opportunity. I just got off the phone with a contact regarding a speaking opportunity. I will be in front of people who know very little about me or my vision, but I am convinced as God gives me opportunities to be in front of people that visibility will open the door to new contacts and new opportunities.

I could write a whole chapter on all the various exposures the Lord has provided that have turned into funding opportunities; instead I'm hoping the Lord will be writing your exciting story of His provision.

Before we move on to step 3, which will help you learn how to categorize your prospective supporters, use the following checklist to make sure you've thoroughly brainstormed as you've listed your prospective supporters.

Prospective Supporters Checklist

Begin to compile your list of prospective donors. Check off each category after you have added the names to your list.

Social media contacts
- [ ] Facebook
- [ ] Twitter
- [ ] LinkedIn
- [ ] other

Church friends
- [ ] friends from home church
- [ ] friends from current church (if different)
- [ ] friends from other churches you have attended

Relatives
- [ ] parents
- [ ] brothers
- [ ] sisters
- [ ] grandparents
- [ ] children
- [ ] aunts/uncles
- [ ] cousins
- [ ] nieces/nephews
- [ ] other

Neighbors
- [ ] former
- [ ] current

School contacts
- [ ] grade school
- [ ] junior high school
- [ ] high school
- [ ] junior college
- [ ] college
- [ ] graduate school

Employment
- [ ] former part-time jobs
- [ ] former full-time jobs
- [ ] current job

Service contacts
- [ ] barber/beautician
- [ ] pediatrician
- [ ] eye doctor
- [ ] other doctor
- [ ] accountant
- [ ] home insurance agent
- [ ] car insurance agent
- [ ] health insurance agent

Service contacts (*continued*)

- [ ] business insurance agent
- [ ] lawyer
- [ ] banker
- [ ] mechanic
- [ ] plumber
- [ ] nursery/preschool aide
- [ ] teacher/babysitter
- [ ] home sales practitioners (Avon, Tupperware, etc.)
- [ ] dry cleaners
- [ ] dentist/orthodontist
- [ ] family doctor
- [ ] surgeon
- [ ] medical specialists
- [ ] Christian bookstore owner
- [ ] contractors
- [ ] auto mechanic
- [ ] others (review the chamber of commerce directories)

Friends

- [ ] your Christmas list
- [ ] your parents' Christmas lists
- [ ] your wedding list (if married)
- [ ] your address book
- [ ] your cell phone contact list
- [ ] your e-mail
- [ ] your family's personal phone book
- [ ] people with whom you've shared hobbies, sports, and other interests

Contacts from your organization

- [ ] missionaries
- [ ] administrators
- [ ] personnel department
- [ ] board members

Friends from other ministries

- [ ] missionaries
- [ ] administrators
- [ ] personnel department
- [ ] board members

Club and civic contacts

- [ ] PTA/PTO
- [ ] neighborhood associations
- [ ] Christian Business Association
- [ ] other (Rotary, Kiwanis, Lions, Optimist)

Miscellaneous

- [ ] companies
- [ ] foundations
- [ ] other

CHAPTER 10

STEP 3: Record, Catalog, and Prioritize Your Prospects

As you gather the names of potential donors from the sources recommended in step 2, organization becomes increasingly important. You will need to record, catalogue, and prioritize the prospective donors and the information you collect about them.

Recording Your List

The best way to record your names is to set up a database using one of many donor software programs. Although new ones are becoming available every day and you may want to explore your options, I can recommend TNT free software (www.tntware.com), Maximizer Technologies (www.maximizer.com), and Act Contact Software (www.Act.com).

As you're tracking information, be as thorough as you can. Here are some of the things I like to track on each prospect or donor:

The Basics
☐ last name
☐ first name
☐ home address
☐ office address
☐ e-mail address
☐ office phone
☐ home phone
☐ cell phone
☐ spouse's name

Additional Information
☐ church
☐ referred by
☐ secretary
☐ profession/position
☐ number of family
   incomes
☐ children
☐ birthdays
☐ anniversaries

☐ hobbies
☐ salutation (titles
   such as Dr., Rev., etc.)
☐ giving interest
☐ giving preference
   (monthly, quarterly,
   annually)

Recognize that all this information will not be available as you begin to build your list, but over a period of time you will discover more about your prospects and donors. It is key to store that for future reference. Keep in mind that we're building relationships with our prospects and donors, and the more information we can obtain about them, the more we can bond with them.

Diary

As I have key conversations by phone and appointments, I maintain a diary to provide me with valuable information as I contact the same people in the future. It would include the date we met. I record any information that will help me to know that prospective donor better—names and ages of their children, giving interests, topics we discussed, what's going on with their jobs.

Cataloging Your Contacts

At this point you should have a good list of contacts and may be beginning the process of gathering and storing that information. To streamline the process, sort your contacts as you go along in a process I call "cataloguing."

Each of your contacts will fall into one of the following categories as seen below:

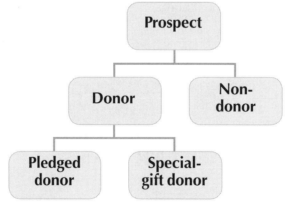

Prospect

Everyone begins as a prospect, a potential supporter of your ministry or organization. Once a prospect is asked for a gift, and you bring that person to a decision, the prospect will then fall into one of two categories, donor or non-donor.

Donor

This category includes all the supporters who were asked for a gift and responded by agreeing to give.

Non-Donor

This category includes contacts whom you asked for a gift, and they decided not to give right now. That "right now" is important. These friends or contacts may be in a position to give in the future. Don't be quick to write them off. A business acquaintance once told me, "A no simply means you are getting closer to a yes."

Pledged Donor

Farther down the chart, you'll notice two types of donors. The pledged donor is a donor who has agreed to give consistently. Of course, this may look different for each person supporting your work. Some donors prefer to give monthly or quarterly, while others may prefer an annual gift. Don't box yourself in by thinking all gifts need to be monthly. It should make little difference to your ministry as long as you know the donor's preference and track the regular giving. Getting a pledge gift is your highest priority. Your prospects and donors need to know that you and your organization operate on a budget so that it is critical that you be able to count on their regular giving.

Special-Gift Donor

You will soon find out not all prospects and donors are wired the same. Many will readily make a pledge, but then along comes the special gift donor, who breaks the mold. This second category of donors includes those who like to respond as the Spirit moves. They hear of a need or catch a vision and quickly respond—until the next vision or need comes along and fires them up. This is not a problem, but be prepared to respond when they choose not to give a pledged gift. This is a perfect opportunity to ask for a special gift. These are donors who can be challenged in the future for additional special gifts. I specifically label these as "special-gift" and not "one-time" donors. If you ask for a one-time gift, the donor who gives once will feel he's done exactly what you asked and is finished. Even worse, you as the fundraiser may feel your work with that person is done. The term "special-gift donor" leaves the door open for future participation and relationship.

Prioritizing Your Contacts

From the start of our journey together in *People Raising*, we've kept the focus on two critical areas:

1. Reducing the fear associated with raising funds
2. Reducing the time it takes to raise needed funds

To accomplish the time-saving goal, I have found it helpful to go through my list of contacts and identify who might be my high-priority, my medium-priority, and my low-priority prospects. Focusing on my high-priority prospects will bring about larger gifts, which will reduce the time the overall fundraising takes.

High-Priority Prospects

High-priority prospects are people who have the financial capability to generously support you or your organization. But the donor's financial cushion is not the only criterion for this category. Donors may be ranked as high-priority based on their eagerness to support you. These donors may have given you signals that they want to be part of your support team.

As you get to know people, you may turn up information that will help you make an educated guess to determine who might be high-priority contacts.

A prospect's *home* can provide a clue. If their home and grounds are extensive, it's quite possible they have the capacity to make a significant gift. If they own more than one home, such as a summer home, that could also be an indicator.

Cars can tell a similar story about their owners' financial cushion.

A prospect's *job* can be an indicator that helps you prioritize, as some positions and industries tend to be more lucrative than others. Find out about your prospect's job, and his or her job title or position. If the prospect is married, are both husband and wife working full-time? Sometimes you will find that a prospective donor owns a business, which can provide freedom for either the individual or the company (or both) to give to your ministry.

Sometimes a prospect will have a source of *extra income*, such as book royalties, or income from property or an inheritance.

Lifestyle can be a significant indicator. Prospects who can spend widely, or who have time for extensive travel, etc., may be open to giving significantly to your ministry.

Don't worry if, as you read these criteria, you find you have few prospects who fall into this category. I am not suggesting any dollar amount, as those can vary. Simply go through your list and identify and bring to the surface those who seem eager to give or who seem to have a higher capacity to give.

Medium-Priority Prospects

Medium-priority prospects are people who may not have great financial capability, yet they need to be asked. Therefore, you will pursue them after you have focused on your high-priority contacts.

Low-Priority Prospects

Low-priority prospects could be people who might support you at a lower amount, or people with whom you have had casual contact.

As you review each name on your list, determine how much you intend to ask of that person. This, obviously, is not a science; you are simply seeking to maximize the prospect's giving potential.

I recommend that you challenge high, which raises the donor's vision. Some wise person has said, "If you aim at nothing, you hit it every time." If you aim low, that's what you'll get. Why ask for $30 per month when a donor might gladly give $150?

Establish a minimum amount you will ask for. I recommend starting with $100. Remember, your prospect can always offer less than the amount of your "ask." Your starting point may be much higher with some high-priority prospects. For example, you might challenge a prospective donor who owns her or her own business to give an annual gift of $5,000.

Be prepared to state a specific amount or a range of possibilities. If you've had a hard time making a guess about what a good target amount is for a specific donor, you might want to offer a range of dollar amounts. If you don't know this donor well, you might want to ask a mutual friend to advise you on what might be a good range.

We will address this issue in detail later in the book. For now, keep in mind that you will rarely embarrass high-priority donors by talking about higher figures. In some cases, you compliment them by asking for a large amount.

Keep in mind that people want to find their place in kingdom work—to discover where they fit in. This is your opportunity to challenge them.

While all prospective supporters may be important to your ministry, I have found that identifying high, medium, and low priorities is essential. It is virtually impossible for you to give equal time to all the people who make up your prospect list. Therefore, you need to identify and spend time with those who will make the biggest impact on you and your ministry.

You may discover contacts who don't really qualify as either high- or medium-priority in terms of financial capability but yet are committed to you in prayer. Be careful not to discount their value to your ministry! Their investment of ongoing prayer support may even be more valuable than financial support.

Two Scenarios

This idea of prioritizing the list could be brand-new and feel foreign and unfamiliar to you. Let me describe two scenarios, one representing the typical approach and the other representing a preferred approach.

Typical Approach

A person takes the growing list of contacts and places the list in alphabetical order, proceeding in the fundraising campaign by going down the list as seen below. Over a period of days and weeks, this fundraiser takes the donors in order, asking the first and second persons on the list for $50 each, and the third for $75, and so on.

Name	Amount	Name	Amount
BJ Bechtel	$50	Bethany LaTorre	$300
Dave Brown	$50	Jeremy Lamour	$300
Julie Bullock	$75	Tisha Lee	$125
Syl Chody	$200	Rusty Lewis	$400
Tiffany Davis	$50	Mark Myers	$500
Brian Dawson	$75	Dick Nordman	$400
Ricky Diaz	$350	Don Raickett	$75
Tony Eager	$150	Brian Relph	$100
Ryan Ernst	$350	Keith Rundquist	$500
Merik Fell	$400	Vanessa Serrano	$400
Bob French	$50	Tyrell Shoemaker	$1000
Edith Greaves	$300	Thad Walker	$150
		Clint Weaks	$600

Preferred Approach

This same fundraiser could have prioritized these donors as H (high), M (medium), or L (low).

L	BJ Bechtel	$50	H	Jeremy Lamour	$300
L	Dave Brown	$50	M	Tisha Lee	$125
L	Julie Bullock	$75	H	Rusty Lewis	$400
M	Syl Chody	$200	H	Mark Myers	$500
L	Tiffany Davis	$50	H	Dick Nordman	$400
L	Brian Dawson	$75	L	Don Raickett	$75
H	Ricky Diaz	$350	L	Brian Relph	$100
M	Tony Eager	$150	H	Keith Rundquist	$500
H	Ryan Ernst	$350	H	Vanessa Serrano	$400
H	Merik Fell	$400	H	Tyrell Shoemaker	$1000
L	Bob French	$50	M	Thad Walker	$150
H	Edith Greaves	$300	H	Clint Weaks	$600
H	Bethany LaTorre	$300			

The fundraiser then focuses on the high-priority prospects.

H	Ricky Diaz	$350	H	Mark Myers	$500
H	Ryan Ernst	$350	H	Dick Nordman	$400
H	Merik Fell	$400	H	Keith Rundquist	$500
H	Edith Greaves	$300	H	Vanessa Serrano	$400
H	Bethany LaTorre	$300	H	Tyrell Shoemaker	$1000
H	Jeremy Lamour	$300	H	Clint Weaks	$600
H	Rusty Lewis	$400			

At the start of fundraising, he may further narrow the focus on the potential Top 10.

H	Tyrell Shoemaker	$1000		H	Rusty Lewis	$400
H	Clint Weaks	$600		H	Dick Nordman	$400
H	Keith Rundquist	$500		H	Vanessa Serrano	$400
H	Mark Myers	$500		H	Ricky Diaz	$350
H	Merik Fell	$400		H	Ryan Ernst	$350

It's obvious that funds will come into your ministry a lot faster as your available time for fundraising is spent by beginning with your top ten contacts. Your ministry is able to operate on the early larger gifts as you pursue medium- and low-priority donor relationships as well.

Focus on your top ten contacts.

But here's a word of caution: Do not begin with these high-priority prospects. I caution you *not* to meet with these high-priority prospects immediately. Read through the book, practice your presentation and how you might respond to donors' questions and objections, and then begin with some of your medium- or low-priority prospects, polishing your presentation before approaching the high-priority prospect.

Use the space below to create your own top-ten list. Remember that every fundraiser's top-ten list will be different and will vary according to their prospects' capacity to give. Those you add could either be prospects or donors. Your top-ten list is going to be very fluid. As you contact these top ten prospects and they make giving decisions, they may move off this list and be replaced by others. It's always great if you encounter new high-priority prospects and have to adjust the list. The point of the exercise is simply to identify those who could make a big difference in your fundraising, as part of the commitment to reducing the time it takes to raise needed funds. This principle alone is huge!

Top Ten Contacts

1. _____

2. _____

3. _____

4. _____

5. _____

6. _____

7. _____

8. _____

9. _____

10. _____

Several years ago I met a young couple who had a love for the Lord's work and were potential givers. I soon ranked them as high-priority, and I devoted time to building our friendship. Today I see in them a couple who not only began giving to our ministry but who have increased their giving. Our friendship has been a blessing on many levels, and I'm grateful now that my system of prioritizing gave me the time necessary to cultivate their friendship.

Initially, the top ten contacts will be from your non-donor prospects list. If you have already raised some support, your Top-ten list may include existing donors. For example, after raising funds for nine months, you may have a donor who has been supporting you from day one. Perhaps recently that person was promoted in his job, and the Lord is blessing him financially. If you sense that you need to contact him again to ask if he will upgrade his pledge, you may move that donor back to your top-ten list.

The Basic Giving Schedule

Another helpful tool is to build a basic giving schedule. This allows you to think through how many people you would need at various levels of support to reach your goal. For example:

xx people @ $500/month

xx people @ $250/month

xx people @ $150/month

xx people @ $100/month

Total monthly goal: $_____

The Pareto principle states that 80 percent of the results flows out of 20 percent of the activity (some promote a 90/10 percent structure). So don't be surprised if 80 percent of your support goal comes from 20 percent of your donors. That scenario could happen. For this reason, focus on your high-priority prospects and challenge that top 20 percent. This 80/20 breakdown is only a principle and not a hard-and-fast rule. So don't get discouraged if you work through 20 percent of your contact list and still haven't met 80 percent of your budget. Trust that God is at work, and keep challenging high.

We will continue to talk about your role in raising the vision of your prospects and donors, but I also hope to raise *your* vision. Don't be afraid to challenge and ask high.

Geography 101

Another way to organize contact information is geographically by zip code. It may be worthwhile for you to travel in person to a given area, if several of your high- and medium-priority contacts live in that area. Make the prearranged appointments, and develop those relationships face-to-face.

Geography comes into play with your own travel or moving plans, as well. If you are going to be traveling through or moving on from a geographical area, maximize your contacts in that area before you move on. For example, a person graduating from college or graduate study should make time to connect with prospects in the area where he or she has been studying—with friends and leaders at the local church, with fellow students and teachers, with work colleagues the student will be leaving behind. Related advice is not to leave your hometown prematurely. Be sure you've had time with your local contacts before you head out to a new ministry locale. Remember, people give to people they know, trust, and care for. These people are more than likely right where you have been living and working.

Making Progress

Does raising funds still seem like climbing an insurmountable mountain? By systematically following the steps outlined in this book, you will find the climb easier. At this point, you've categorized a list of potential donors. You should have identified your Top 10. You will want to focus your energies with the hope of the best return on your investment of time and energy. Begin to pray for these top ten individuals.

You have already come a long way. You have recognized that it is biblical to seek funds. You have started the ball rolling with your church, and you have built, catalogued, and prioritized your list. It is now time to get the word out.

CHAPTER 11

STEP 4:
Get the Word Out

In the good old days, which was not that long ago, communication mostly meant you drafted a letter and put it in the mail. Today, thanks to the Internet, you have many ways of letting your friends and contacts know of your call to ministry.

You must get the word out about your ministry or organization, but there is not only one way, or method, for accomplishing this. In fact, the methods you use to communicate about your ministry are going to be intensely personal, depending largely on the prospective donors on your list. The key is to consider specific people to determine the best ways of communicating with them. You probably are already communicating with some by Facebook, Twitter, texting, e-mail, letter, or phone. With others, you may very well be implementing more than one medium to interact.

Your goal is to communicate, and you will need to do it in whatever medium is most comfortable for your donor and not necessarily what is most convenient for you. You may be Internet savvy and proficient at texting, but some of your donors will prefer a letter followed by a phone call.

Even though you have created and organized your donor list, this step about acquainting contacts with your ministry is *not* about money or asking for funds. Getting the word out sets the stage for future fundraising. Remember that *Harvard Business Review* study about effective forms of communication? While that particular study did not include e-mail, Facebook, and other Internet social media, they ranked these forms of communication in the following order:

1.	One-on-one
2.	Small group discussion
3.	Large group discussion
4.	Telephone
5.	Handwritten letter
6.	Typed letter
7.	Mass letter
8.	Newsletter
9.	Brochure
10.	News item
11.	Advertisement
12.	Handout

Whatever form you use, I encourage you to not take shortcuts. Efficiency is nice, but effectiveness is essential. In other words, don't go sit down at your computer, pull up Facebook, and immediately shoot out requests to every contact you've ever had, thinking, "Cool! Look how fast I can get to asking for support!" That sure does sound efficient, but effectiveness is the goal—and a Facebook post is not going to be your most effective fundraising method.

The most effective approach in fundraising is personal contact—one-on-one. So step 4, getting the word out, is a preliminary stage in the fundraising strategy. You get the word out now, and follow up in the future.

That is why at this stage you only want to get the word out and follow up as we lay out the strategy.

What to Communicate

As you craft this earliest communication for your contacts, here are some of the things you might *briefly* want to get across:

Your vision

Your call

Your assignment—duties and location

Your excitement

Your organization

Your need for prayer

Your need to raise funds

Your timetable

Your desire to continue to communicate

So the sky is the limit on what methods you will use to get out this early word about your organization or ministry.

Another effective tool is to have your organization provide a letter of introduction.

[Date]
[Address]

Dear Friend,

What a joy it is for me to inform you that Rodney and Tammi Smith have been accepted for overseas service with Mission Aviation Fellowship, with appointment to the Democratic Republic of Congo. We warmly welcome them into our MAF missionary family and anticipate their contribution to our ministry team. I hope you will take time to hear the story of God's direction and the passion of their heart to serve the Lord with MAF.

My desire is to see this gifted couple placed in a position that will maximize their service for Christ and fulfill His will for their lives. As God has provided the talent and skills for the task, I believe He will also supply everything Rodney and Tammi need to serve in the Democratic Republic of Congo. I invite you to join us in praying that those of God's choosing will join hands with them to provide the needed ministry support to carry out this service to Christ. Would you prayerfully consider being one to join with them? As you are invited to become a prayer and financial partner in their ministry, please ask God what your role should be.

During these next few months Rodney and Tammi will be sharing their ministry with churches and friends. MAF has assigned Jean Wunsch, Ministry Partnership counselor, to assist, encourage, and hold them accountable during their deputation ministry. If Jean can help you in any way, or answer any questions, please write or call at [list ministry number].

We have enclosed introductory material about Rodney and Tammi—for you, or to pass on to someone else who may be interested. Additional copies are available as needed. Perhaps you could refer Rodney and Tammi to others, thus opening a door of opportunity for them.

It would be a real advantage to Rodney and Tammi to have the individuals and churches desiring to support their ministry begin giving now. Should you desire any further information, please let us know.

Thank you for your interest and concern for Rodney and Tammi. We look forward to your partnership with them.

Very sincerely in Him,
John Boyd
Chief Executive Officer [1]

Later in the deputation process, your mission agency may provide an update on your financial support and needs. For those who have not responded but have shown interest, this progress report may help them decide to become involved, either with a special gift or with ongoing support. Here's one mailed by a mission on behalf of Mike and Isobel.

[Date]
[Address]

Dear Friend,

We promised to keep you posted on the progress of Mike and Isobel, and several months have now passed by. These have been busy and at times faith-testing days for them. But they have also been exciting days as they've watched God answer prayers! Thank you for the encouragement your prayers have brought.

Concerning their financial needs, they have reached the 65% mark in promised ministry support, but $1,400 monthly is still lacking. Outgoing expenses are still needed. These include pre-field salary and related expenses $24,401; travel to Zaire $3,800; shipping $5,600; language school $3,000 and passports, visas, customs, etc. $1,000. Until their monthly support and outgoing expenses are met in full, the field budget will experience constraints that determine whether the opportunities before them can be fully met.

If God is challenging you to become involved with Mike and Isobel, now would be the perfect time to let them know by completing the form below and returning it to us as soon as possible. Let's pray that these financial needs may soon be cared for. Thank you for your interest in this dedicated family.

Sincerely in Christ,

(Mrs.) Phyllis Beiter
Ministry Partnership[2]

( ) I will help send Mike and Isobel Dunkley to their assignment in Zaire by committing:
$_____per month $_____per quarter $_____per year in support of their ministry.

( ) I am enclosing a special gift of $_____ for their outgoing expenses.

Now that you've got the word out, your next step is to call and set up some appointments. The next chapter will help you get well prepared.

CHAPTER 12

STEP 5:
Make Appointments

Remember that people give to people they know and trust and care about. Knowing that one-on-one visits provide the best way for people to get to know and trust you, the next step is to make appointments with your prospective donors. What is it that makes the personal interaction so effective in fundraising? Let's identify the value of meeting one-on-one.

You have another person's undivided attention.
Meeting allows for two-way communication.
Your time and attention communicate that you value the contact.
Your effort signals you have something important to share.

Here are some of the goals you want to accomplish through the appointment.

- To build your relationship
- To share your vision
- To provide your prospects an opportunity to give
- To develop prayer partners

The goal of each phone call is to get the appointment, not to tell your whole story. If you take the opportunity by phone to tell your whole story, you might find your prospect saying something like, "I believe you have done a good job of bringing me up to date. I don't think there is any need for us to get together."

Some of you might readily be able to secure an appointment through texting, e-mail, Facebook, or other social media, but I still put in my vote for the phone. It is a lot easier for your prospect to quickly respond by social media and say no and not give you the opportunity to respond to their objections. A phone conversation can turn a "No, we don't really want to meet" to "Okay, let's get together." Remember, your goal is to get the appointment.

Making the Phone Calls

Precede each call with prayer. If when you reach for the phone you find your heart pounding and hands sweating, welcome to the club. Calling for fundraising purposes can be scary, but many times I have lived beyond the fear, made the calls, and ended up with supporters who became part of my team. It was worth it!

Get the appointment; don't tell your whole story.

Pray that you will speak the right words and be sensitive as you talk. Pray for openness in those whom you call. Pray that God will work beyond your strategy to accomplish His will.

Remember, you are not making cold calls but calling people you know. Begin by calling people you believe will be most receptive. You need some wins under your belt. You need to know that making the call was not so bad after all. When I feel nervous, it helps me to call people I think will be receptive. Once I have successfully made those calls, I gain some courage for the more difficult calls.

If you are married, be sure to have your spouse make the calls to the prospects on your list who come from his or her family, friends, or colleagues. Since people give to those they know and trust and care about, it's important for the partner who has the most significant relationship with the prospective donor to initiate the contact.

As you make the call, simply assume that prospective donors want to meet with you, and give them a choice of times. For example, say, "I really would like to meet with you. Would it be better this week or next week?" Or, "I would like to get together with you. Would you prefer Monday or Friday?" There is an old sales adage that instructs, "Don't ask 'If,' ask 'Which.'" "May I see you tomorrow?" leaves you more vulnerable than "What time can I see you tomorrow?"

Practice prior to your call. Adapt your phone script using words that feel comfortable and sound like you, using phrases that will best help you secure an appointment. When you have the script down pat, you will speak with more confidence.

When one of our ICI staff was having difficulty securing appointments, I asked, "Tell me what you say when you get on the phone."

He answered, "I say that I have just returned from college. I plan to be a missionary; I would like to meet with you."

I reminded this young fundraiser that wording makes a difference. I encouraged him to try this approach: "I'm very excited about the ministry the Lord has called me to, and I really want to meet with you. Would this week or next week be better?" Wording is important!

Helpful Hints

Be sure when somebody answers your call that you are talking to the right person. There is nothing more embarrassing than talking at length and then hearing, "Maybe you ought to talk to my dad."

Be positive and sincere. Expect people to want to meet with you.

Show enthusiasm. Let people know you are excited. Smile as you talk.

Be brief and concise.

Avoid phoning at inconvenient times. For example, avoid calling families in the morning when Mom and Dad are getting the kids off to school. Avoid phoning at mealtimes. And it is usually not best to call late into the evening.

If you sense you are calling at an inconvenient time simply ask when you can call back. When you return the call, create an environment in which you can get a positive response.

When you have had success, make another call immediately. You are likely to be more effective after successfully setting an appointment. When you are on a roll, keep calling.

Scheduling the Meeting

When Will You Meet?

Consideration for your prospective donors is more important than your personal convenience, so stay flexible and try to work around other people's schedules. Be prepared to meet when your donors want to meet.

But you may, of course, suggest meeting times. Busy people might prefer to schedule an appointment around a meal. You might split a day into these six time slots: breakfast, mid-morning, lunch, mid-afternoon, dinner, early evening.

Where Will You Meet?

Flexibility is also crucial when it comes to the meeting place. Be prepared to go where your prospects or donors are or to meet where they prefer to meet.

One of our ICI staff called a prospective donor and got the typical response: "I am too busy." My staff member did not take no for a quick answer and immediately generated another option: He met the donor on his construction site. That busy man, who could not find twenty minutes to get away from work for an appointment, gave our staff member a big chunk of his time on the job site. To this day that busy worker continues to support our staff member.

The ideal meeting place offers few distractions and provides you the opportunity to talk at length, if needed. For example, talking while standing in the church hallway does not give you the time to talk seriously. Instead, set a definite place and time for an appointment.

If you are approaching a couple, try to meet with both of them. Think how discouraging it will be if you meet with the wife and she gets excited about your ministry but then is unable to convince her husband to support you. You need to meet with both decision makers.

In a few cases, it may be wise to meet with just one marriage partner. For example, one spouse might be very committed to giving while the other feels threatened. Or, occasionally, only one spouse makes all the financial decisions.

How Long Will You Meet?

There is no magical time frame. A busy professional might only give you twenty minutes, while meeting with a close friend might call for an extended meeting time so that you both can relax, take time to catch up with each other, go into detail, and make the request for support (what fundraisers call "the ask").

Basic Phone Script

I highly recommend developing a basic phone script and practicing ahead of time, so that it begins to feel natural for you. Here's how a phone call might go:

Identify yourself.

This is fundamental telephone etiquette. I might say, "This is Bill Dillon from Inner City Impact in Chicago. Is Bob Smith in?"

Get the right person.

Be sure you have the right person on the line. Remember, in the case of couples, you need to decide in advance which spouse you want to ask for the appointment, but seek the opportunity meet both in person.

Engage in general conversation.

Since you are mainly phoning people you know, begin at a natural point in your friendship. Pick up where you left off with this friend in your last conversation. You might find yourself talking about family, career, church, mutual friends, hobbies, weather, or current events. Identify a similar experience that you both share to develop rapport. What do you have in common?

Adapt your phone presentation, tone, and pace to put your phone partner at ease. When a prospective donor is reserved, respect that by taking a more formal, reserved approach. If your prospective donor is upbeat, try to join with your friend in spirit and tone. This connection is sometimes called "vocal matching."[1]

State the reason for your call.

Your agenda for a meeting is to share your vision as well as to solicit support for your organization or ministry. You might say, "The Lord has called me into ministry, and I am anxious to meet with you and tell you more about the details of my work and the vision the Lord has given me. Also I want to share ways people can participate financially."

You must mention the money issue. If you make an appointment and allow your prospective donor to think your upcoming meeting is simply a social call, the donor may feel blindsided by your request for support. So it is critical you mention money and then back off that subject. This isn't the time to mention dollar amounts or go on and on about your financial needs. The goal is simply to make the appointment, while being up front regarding what the meeting is about.

Ask for the appointment.

Seek a time to meet in person, keeping in mind the advice about offering the prospect or donor options of time and place. You might say, "I really would like to meet with you. Would it be better this week or next week?"

Finalize details.

Cover the bases, confirming date and time and directions. You might say,

"That's great. I will see you at 6:00 p.m. next Friday, September 17, at your home. Your home address is 2251 Pine—is that correct? Will you give me directions from the expressway?"

Wrap up your conversation.

Keep your good-byes personal and courteous, in keeping with the tone that the donor has set in the conversation. Reiterate your eagerness for the meeting: "Sure looking forward to being with you. See you next Friday."

Calling Busy Professionals

In setting appointments with busy people, be patient. Don't be discouraged when your prospect does not agree to see you within your time frame. Be persistent. Take good notes and place on your calendar a reminder to yourself when you should call again.

Don't assume that a put-off means rejection. A busy person lives on a fast track, and you need to recognize that a prospect or donor may really want to see you, but it will take time to fit you into his or her demanding schedule.

Remember, the goal of your phone call is to set up an appointment. If you don't get an appointment, you will miss the opportunity to raise their vision and challenge them to be part of your team. Be persistent in pursuing a busy person. Work hard to create options. Suggest other dates. Don't give up!

I prefer to speak with my prospects in person, so I don't always leave my name with a receptionist or administrative assistant. I don't want to annoy my donor contacts or appear to be too pushy. Often I just tell the person on the other end of the line that I'll be glad to call at another time, and I ask when might be a better time to call.

I tend to avoid calling busy people on Monday mornings, when the workweek is just getting into swing and the day can be exhausting or hectic. You might also want to avoid phoning late on a Friday afternoon, when professional people may be hoping to get things wrapped up so they can get away from the office and begin the weekend.

I have had busy professionals express the heavy demands on their personal calendar:

"Bill, I can't meet next week—I will be on business in New York. The following week I will be in Los Angeles. Next month I am preparing for our annual meeting. Then I am going on a golf outing down South, followed by a family vacation."

This hard worker is under a serious amount of schedule stress, but that doesn't mean this prospective donor will never want to hear about my ministry. So I would respond with understanding by saying, "I know you are extremely busy. It sounds like we need to set a date for two months from now. Is there a date we can set now, or should I phone then?"

The key is to end your conversation with a date set for you to call again. But don't be surprised when you call in six weeks and that busy professional is out of town. You may have to try numerous times before you can speak with him again.

You will probably feel tempted to think such an elusive prospective donor is not interested in supporting your ministry. But don't allow negative thinking to discourage you. The heavy work and travel schedule may simply be that prospect's everyday reality; his life really is that hectic. Your persistence and pleasant follow-through can make the difference, and it may build a relationship with a person who may not have a lot of time for friendship apart from the job.

> *Persistence and pleasant follow-through can make the difference, and it may build a relationship.*

Personal assistants can be helpful in suggesting times to reach their bosses by phone. I tried to contact one man on numerous occasions. His assistant finally said, "He leaves by noon most days." When I asked what time he got in to the office, she replied, "Seven a.m." So I called just after 7:00 a.m. and got through to him directly.

Listen as people share their schedules. One day I had a phone conversation with a man who mentioned that he is always in his office on Fridays to meet with his staff. I made a note of this fact in my contact diary and then made it a practice to call him on Fridays. I always get through to him.

Avoid the tendency to give up on making a personal appointment. Potential donors need to look you in the eye, see your passion for the ministry, ask you questions, and understand your vision more fully.

Confirmation

In many cases it is wise to confirm the appointment. You might do it by phone, email, text, Facebook or, for a business professional, you might confirm the appointment by sending a letter like the one included here. Send the reminder letter the day you set the appointment, including both the day of the week and the date on the calendar of the meeting you have agreed on together.

Dear _____,

It was good talking by phone today. I appreciate your willingness to meet to learn more about my ministry.

We live in a time of unprecedented opportunity to share Christ. I am anxious to get together and share how the Lord has been leading in my life.

Thanks again for your interest. I'm looking forward to meeting you on [date and day of appointment] at [time of appointment] at [place of appointment].

Sincerely,

Handling Objections

By now you have a good idea of how to approach prospective supporters and how to make appointments. But it's also important for you to have prepared in advance how to repond to a prospect's possible objections to a meeting. In this section, we will look at several types of objections and appropriate responses.

As you seek appointments, count on the fact that individuals will have objections. Handling those objections can be the hardest part of raising funds. Getting past them is essential.

You deal with objections in two steps: (1) Respond to the objection. It is real in the mind of the prospect. (2) Ask for the appointment again.

A professional with a demanding schedule may object, saying, "I work downtown. I leave at 5:30 a.m. and don't get home until 7:30 p.m."

You respond to the objection (part A): "I know you are extremely busy, but I would be more than happy to arrange my schedule to meet you downtown."

You ask for the appointment again (part B): "How about lunch downtown next Wednesday or Friday?"

Respond to the objection. Ask for the appointment again.

Your positive response has created other options.

Responding quickly and naturally to objections takes practice. So it is important that you role-play with a coach or friend. Using this list, have this friend call out an objection, and you follow immediately with a two-part response that responds to the objection (which is real in the mind of the prospect) and also requests the appointment again. Suggestions for responding are given below. Practice until responding becomes second nature for you.

Objection: "I am already giving to other individuals or organizations. There really is no need for us to meet."

Objection: "We heard your presentation at church Sunday evening, and we feel we already know quite a bit about your ministry."

Objection: "I am too busy to meet with you."

Objection: "What is the purpose of our meeting?"

Objection: "Is this about finances?"

Objection: "Why do you want to meet with me?"

Objection: "We know the church is supporting you, so we don't see the need to get together."

Objection: "I am not interested in meeting with you, and I am sorry but I cannot be an encouragement to you."

Objection: *"I am already giving to other individuals or organizations. There really is no need for us to meet."*

I love to meet with people who already love to give. If they catch my vision and passion, many of them will find a way to give. Don't be discouraged by the overcommitted donor. Your natural response is to agree that perhaps he is too committed to help. However, I would rather speak to an overcommitted donor than to a non-donor who has never experienced the joy of giving.

Recognize that the stronger your relationship with a prospect, the easier it will be to get an appointment. Those who have little relationship with you will be harder. But you must insist on meeting people one-on-one! Don't take a shortcut by asking for a financial commitment over the phone.

Part A: Respond to the objection: "I can understand that, but I am anxious to update you on what the Lord has been doing in my life and my plans for the future."

Part B: Ask for the appointment again: "I would love the opportunity to meet with you. Would Monday next week be good or would Wednesday be better?"

Objection: *"We heard your presentation at church Sunday evening, and we feel we already know quite a bit about your ministry."*

Remember to respond to their real objection, and then to provide options.

Respond to the objection: "I am so glad you were there and could get acquainted with our ministry, but I want to give you an update and go into more detail about what the Lord has been doing in my life."

Ask for the appointment again: "Would a breakfast be good, or do you prefer to meet over lunch?"

Objection: *"I am too busy to meet with you."*

Respond to the objection: "I can understand that you are extremely busy. But I would be happy to have just twenty minutes of your time so I can tell you about the burden and vision the Lord has given me."

Ask for the appointment again: "How about twenty minutes next Wednesday or Friday?"

If a prospective supporter agrees to give you twenty minutes, stick to twenty minutes. As you get toward the end of your twenty minutes, you might courteously ask if the prospect will give you some additional time. But be prepared to honor your commitment to stick to twenty minutes.

Objection: *"What is the purpose of our meeting?"*
Objection: *"Is this about finances?"*
Objection: *"Why do you want to meet with me?"*

For each of these questions, you can **respond to the objection** in a similar way: "I really want to tell you about the vision the Lord has given me and explain some details of the work to which the Lord has called me. I certainly will be prepared to share some of the opportunities for prayer and financial involvement but the meeting is more than money."

Ask for the appointment again: "How does Tuesday or Thursday look on your schedule?"

Objection: *"We know the church is supporting you, so we don't see the need to get together."*

Many prospective supporters will probably think the church really is undertaking the majority of your support. It is time for you to do some educating, helping prospects understand the whole picture of your need and that you need additional people to meet your goal.

Part A: Respond to the objection: "We are so grateful for the church. We are required to raise $4000 a month and so appreciate the church's commitment of $500."

Part B: Ask for the appointment again: "I would love to meet. Are weekdays better or weekends?"

Objection: *"I am not interested in meeting with you; I am sorry but I cannot be an encouragement to you."*

Part A: Respond to the objection: "I can understand that. Thanks for taking the time to talk. I certainly could use your prayer support as I seek to respond to the challenge the Lord has given me. I will keep you aware of some of my prayer needs."

Such a frank statement of disinterest closes the door, for now, regarding an appointment. However, do keep this prospect on your list to receive your ministry updates.

It is extremely important that you role-play your response to these objections. You need to be prepared to counteract any potential objections. Missionary Aviation Fellowship of Canada offers the following two charts to help you handle phone objections and for keeping track of your efforts.

Handling Phone Objections

1	2	3	4
Very Busy **Will be out of town** **Bad time right now**	**Does this have to do with money?**	**I already give to** **_____.**	**Not interested!**
I can understand that. These are busy times. Perhaps I can get back in touch with you when it is more convenient for you. How about...?	Well, part of it will be about money, but most of it will be informational. Of course, there is no obligation involved and I am sure you will be encouraged to hear about all the Lord is doing through [name of your ministry].	It is not my intention to detract you from your current involvement in any way. I would really like the opportunity to meet with you and tell you some of the things that are happening with [name of your ministry]. I am sure you would be encouraged to hear about all that the Lord is doing.	I can appreciate your feelings. You know, there is another way in which you can help me, if you would. I am asking people if they might be willing to pray for my ministry from time to time. Do you think that I could occasionally send you my personal prayer letters so that you can keep up to date on what is going on in the ministry?

Weekly Support Team Development Chart

Name _____Sat._____to Fri._____Week #_____

Your Goal	Guide-lines	Area	Actual (circle as you process)											
_____	225	Calls made (i.e., number of times you dial the phone)	1	2	3	4	5	6	7	8	9	10	11	12
			13	14	15	16	17	18	19	20	21	22	23	24
			25	26	27	28	29	30	31	32	33	34	35	36
			37	38	39	40	41	42	43	44	45	46	47	48
			49	50	51	52	53	54	55	56	57	58	59	60
			61	62	63	64	65	66	67	68	69	70	71	72
			73	74	75	76	77	78	79	80	81	82	83	94
			85	86	87	88	89	90	91	92	93	94	95	96
			97	98	99	100	101	102	103	104	105	106	107	108
			109	110	111	112	113	114	115	116	117	118	119	120
			121	122	123	124	125	126	127	128	129	130	131	132
			133	134	135	136	137	138	139	140	141	142	143	144
			145	146	147	148	149	150	151	152	153	154	155	156
			157	158	159	160	161	162	163	164	165	166	167	168
			169	170	171	172	173	174	175	176	177	178	179	180
			181	182	183	184	185	186	187	188	189	190	191	192
			193	194	195	196	197	198	199	200	201	202	203	204
			205	206	207	208	209	210	211	212	213	214	215	216
			217	218	219	220	221	222	223	224	225			
_____	45	People talked to	1	2	3	4	5	6	7	8	9	10	11	12
			13	14	15	16	17	18	19	20	21	22	23	24
			25	26	27	28	29	30	31	32	33	34	35	36
			37	38	39	40	41	42	43	44	45	46	47	48
			49	50										
_____	22	Appointments set up	1	2	3	4	5	6	7	8	9	10	11	12
			13	14	15	16	17	18	19	20	21	22	23	24
			25	26	27	28	29	30						
_____	0	Appointments kept	1	2	3	4	5	6	7	8	9	10	11	12
			13	14	15	16	17	18	19	20	21	22	23	24
			25	26	27	28	29	30						
_____	0	Appointments not kept	1	2	3									
_____	10	New ministry partners	1	2	3	4	5	6	7	8	9	10	11	12
			13	14	15	16	17	18	19	20				
_____	$200 weekly target	New monthly	5	10	15	20	25	30	35	40	45	50	55	60
			65	70	75	80	85	90	95	100	105	110	115	120
			125	130	135	140	145	150	155	160	165	170	175	180
			185	190	195	200	205	210	220	230	240	245	250	255
_____	$400-500 weekly target	New special needs	50	100	150	200	250	300	350	400	450	500	550	600
			650	700	750	800	850	900	950	1000				

Troubleshooting Your Phone Calls for Appointments

Missionary Aviation Fellowship has provided the following analysis of causes and solutions of low areas in support-raising.[2]

A "low area" is defined as "one that is significantly lower than the guidelines listed on the chart" on p. 107. For example, if you talk to thirty people about an appointment, about half, or fifteen, people should set up appointments with you. So if you talk to thirty people and only seven make appointments, then you should look under "Few appointments set" for a possible cause and solution.

LOW AREA: *Few calls made*

Possible cause	Laziness
Solution	Pray for enthusiasm about the opportunity to help others become a part of your ministry. Start moving and trusting God for the results.

Possible cause	Lack of contacts to call
Solution	Ask each of your contacts for referrals. Stimulate a prospective donor's thinking by asking for names of members of his Sunday school class or if he has a church directory he will go through with you. That may give you thirty to forty contacts.

Possible cause	Fear
Solution	Pray for courage. Remind yourself that you are doing potential donors a great favor to give them the opportunity to become a part of a people-changing ministry. Set definite times to sit at the phone and make calls.

LOW AREA: *Few people talked to*

Possible cause	Calling at bad times of the day
Solution	Most professionals are at home after supper (7:00–9:30 p.m.).

Possible cause	Don't know how to get to a spouse
Solution	Ask the husband or wife for the best time to catch the person. Also ask for an office or cell number. Check with a receptionist or personal assistant for the best time to reach him.

LOW AREA: *Few appointments set*

Possible cause	Not following prepared script
Solution	Start reading it!

Possible cause	Not speaking with enthusiasm
Solution	Ask God to make you enthusiastic. Practice reading the script with enthusiasm. After reading it fifty times it may seem canned to you, but it is fresh for each contact.

LOW AREA: *Appointments not being kept*

Possible cause	If a person does not show or forgets an appointment, you may not have sent a reminder or made the time clear.
Solution	Send a reminder e-mail or letter, clearly stating appointment date, day, time, and place.

Possible cause	If you forget a meeting or are late, you may not be keeping an accurate appointment book, or you are not leaving previous appointments soon enough.
Solution	Keep an accurate appointment book. Map your route the night before, so you know where to go, how to get there, and when to leave one appointment to get to your next one.

Remember, few people will call you to set up an appointment. You are the one who needs to ask for their time. I assure you that you will enjoy connecting or reconnecting with people. It's all about People Raising. The following chapter will thoroughly equip you to conduct those visits.

CHAPTER 13

STEP 6:
Conduct the Visit

You have got the appointment, and you feel pretty good about that. But then all of a sudden you are struck by a new fear. You say to yourself, *What am I going to say? How do I begin? When do I ask for the gift? If they want to pray about it, what do I say?*

I am with you, having experienced all these reservations myself. But I am confident you can prepare in advance and be ready for productive one-on-one visits with your prospects or donors.

Preparing for the Visit

The time has come to venture forth from the comforts of your home or apartment into the "real world." It's time to actually meet with people—the heart and best part of fundraising. It's time to become better acquainted with other members of the body of Christ and to build relationships.

If you are scared or at least apprehensive, join the club. Making a personal visit can be challenging yet it can be extremely satisfying.

Several years ago, I was asked to speak to the board of directors of a Christian ministry. As I stressed the importance of asking for a financial gift, a board member interrupted me to say, "Mr. Dillon, you don't understand. I get nervous, my heart begins to race, and my hands begin to sweat."

I interrupted her to say, "Ma'am, you have just described Bill Dillon. I get nervous, too, and it's natural to have those times when the heart begins to race."

I'll say it again: I am committed to reducing the fear in fundraising, but there is no way to completely eliminate it.

One of the best ways to reduce the fear of an anticipated face-to-face meeting with a prospect is to prepare for it.

Appearance

Dress appropriately. Dress for your audience. For a business call, you will want to dress professionally. For men, that might mean a dress shirt and tie with a suit or sport coat. But find out the office policy of the business you are visiting. Call in advance to determine the company "dress code." If they have a casual business atmosphere, you will want to dress so that you and the prospect both feel comfortable.

When you take the time to dress to fit the occasion, you communicate that you value the meeting you're going to have, and you show respect for your prospect.

The bottom line is to look presentable.

Breath/Body Odor

It would be a shame to put off the receptivity of a prospective donor simply because it's a hot day and you failed to prepare adequately to restrain the smells that come with body odor. It seems like a basic instruction, but use your deodorant and appropriate, not overwhelming, perfumes or colognes.

I always carry breath mints and recommend that you do the same. Your appointment may include a meeting at the prospect's favorite pizza joint, and it's good to be prepared.

Directions

Go over your directions in advance, and don't rely solely on GPS. Keep the prospect's phone number handy just in case you are delayed. Allow sufficient travel time so that you arrive relaxed and confident. Racing into an appointment late or in the nick of time does not make a good impression. If you arrive early, either spend a few minutes in the car or a lobby, praying before your meeting. In some cases, it may be possible that your prospect will be able to start the meeting earlier, if you are there in advance of your time.

Goal

The goal of your meeting is to ask the prospect or donor to support you with their financial gifts and prayers. Therefore, it is important to be highly focused in your visit and move them to a decision.

Time

Your appointments may be as brief as twenty minutes with a busy professional or as long as two hours with a close friend. To accomplish your goal in twenty minutes,

> *The goal of your meeting is to ask a potential donor to support you.*

you must be brief and concise. That will require discipline and practice. Wear a watch, or keep an eye on a clock. Be courteous about respecting the time the prospect has agreed to give you.

Review

Review whatever information you have about your prospect—a spouse's name and the names of other family members, family background, church, work, hobbies, and interests. Review what each prospect may be able to give financially.

Go over what you intend to tell the prospect about your organization and your sense of calling and your need. If your ministry has a brochure or something else for you to give your prospect, have that ready. Remind yourself of the dollar amount or dollar range you intend to use as a basis for this "ask."

List Projects

The prospect may indicate to you that rather than give monthly or annually, he would be interested in becoming a special-gift donor. Ahead of time, prepare a list of special, specific needs that you might have. Estimate a specific dollar amount for each project.

Moving costs	$ _____
Ministry start-up	$ _____
Training/education	$ _____
Vehicle need	$ _____
Medical need	$ _____

Think in terms of specific projects, in case that turns out to be this prospect's preferred giving style.

Pack

Bring whatever necessary literature, pledge cards, prayer cards, business reply envelope, DVD, and notebooks you will need.

Relax

Put yourself in a positive mood. Your mood and actions affect others; prospects or donors will respond to your mood. If you display friendliness, sincerity, and warmth, they are likely to react the same way. Therefore, presenting yourself in a calm, competent, and relaxed manner is important. Relax, knowing that the person set the appointment because he is interested in what you are doing.

Pray

Pray! Pray! Pray! There is no better way to relax your mind and gather your courage than to pray before going into your appointment. Pray for courage, wisdom, and that all will go well. You are presenting the Lord's business. He who calls you will provide for you. It's His work and His ministry. Do your best, and then leave the outcome in the Lord's hands.

Opening

Be prepared with opening phrases as you meet at the door. "It is so good to see you again. I have been looking forward to getting together."

Setting

As you walk into the office or home, take a quick look at the surroundings. A special picture, award, or object may suggest a special interest that the prospect has and a possible topic for conversation. For example, if the home is decorated with Western art, you might talk about that. If they have a special collection, ask basic questions: "How long have you been collecting?" "How did you get into collecting?"

When walking into the room in which you meet, allow your host to seat himself or herself first. Then position yourself close by so you can converse with them. If you brought items to look at, you might suggest sitting around a table.

Six Word Pictures to Guide Your Presentation

After you and your prospect are seated, and you've engaged in some brief, informal communication, you will naturally begin the conversation about your work and ministry.

If you are like me—and almost everyone else—you need a plan. You'll need to have organized ahead of time how you intend to begin, how you'll wrap up the meeting—and how many steps you'll take in between. Thousands of people who have looked to People Raising for practical training and advice find six steps most helpful.

To help you memorize these six steps, you need only remember six word pictures, in sequence. Use your imagination to picture yourself in this scenario:

1. In your left hand is a photo *album.*
2. In your right hand is a road *map.*
3. On a table is a *globe.*
4. On the table are some reading *glasses.*
5. On the table is a *blueprint.*
6. Beyond the table is a group of people dressed in *uniforms* with your name across them.

Album

The photo album in your left hand represents an update of your life. As you begin the meeting, bring the prospect or donor up to date with your life. Think of the photo album as organized by year. Go back where you left off with the friendship and tell the prospect about your activities and goals from that time until now. Also get caught up on the prospect's life; there's no need to focus only on you.

Map

The road map in your right hand represents how God has led you into ministry. Tell your story of how you got to this point.

Globe

The globe on the table represents world missions. Talk about your organization or work and how it fits into world evangelization. People need to know you are not just venturing out on your own but are connected with a well-respected organization. Have the necessary details about your organization to share.

Reading Glasses

The reading glasses represent your vision. Talk about what you believe God is calling you to do. Get excited as you share. This is a key bit of advice: talk vision, not need. Don't focus on the fact you need a salary and benefits. Focus on what you want to accomplish for the Lord.

> *Prepare your photo album, globe, map, glasses, blueprint, and uniforms.*

Blueprint

The blueprint represents your financial plan. Just as a building requires blueprints, you also need a plan to raise needed ministry funds. Talk about your plan for raising the funds. For example, you might say, "I am seeking the support of my home church and have identified friends I plan to go to so I can see my financial goal met."

Uniforms

The people in uniforms with your name represent those who have joined your support team through their giving and prayer. How do people get on your support team? You ask them. This is the point in your presentation when you ask the prospect to join your team. Your goal is to bring them to a decision.

The Actual Visit

With those six word pictures in mind to help you remember a simple outline for your meeting, write out and practice a fleshed-out version of the presentation, according to the outline, so that it becomes second nature. Find a coach or mentor, and role-play an entire visit a number of times before you make your first visit.

The Photo Album: Bring the Person Up-to-Date with Your Life

Some people you visit may not have seen you for months or even years. So start where you left off. For example, if the last time you saw this prospect was during your sophomore year of high school, you may want to begin with finishing high school, then review your college and work experiences and other significant events that have taken place in your life up until today.

Then get up-to-date on your friend's life. Use the following questions as guidelines:

"Since we met or talked last what has happened in terms of your career?"
"Tell me about your family/children."
"How have you been involved in your church?"
"Have you developed any hobbies?"
"How do you use your free time?"

The key is to listen, listen, and listen. As you listen, you will learn more about the person—his or her family, interests, and personal needs. This will make you a better friend and will allow you to better pray for and minister to this prospective donor.

When I called one prospective donor, he asked how I was and how the ministry was going. I talked about my ministry and asked him how his business and family were. Then he revealed that his wife had just asked for a divorce. I was ready to listen and to minister.

If you have prepared and role-played the visit in advance, you will be relaxed and able to listen. You will not be preoccupied with what to say. So do your homework, and practice.

Recognize that people will respond to you in different ways. You will encounter different personality types.

The Expressive. Meeting with people and talking is enjoyable for them. Because they enjoy talking, they will probably talk a great deal before you have an opportunity to jump in. Listen patiently, and maintain sincere interest.

The Aggressive. This person will take charge and begin to ask questions about your ministry and involvement, often because they are curious. They will control the conversation.

When it is necessary to make a transition into section 2, the following phrase may be helpful: "Glad you asked. That brings me to my next point—"

The Suppressive. These good listeners leave it to you to take charge of the conversation. They will wait without giving you any indication of what is on their minds. But they are ready to listen.

If conversational skills don't come easily to you, you may want to practice cue lines that keep a conversation moving:

"Could you tell me about—?"

"How did you do that—?"

"What did you do when—?"

"How did you feel about—?"

"You mean—, they did that—? Then what happened?"

Sometimes when you're listening, the conversation moves along better with a limited response from you. These listening recognition sounds keep the conversation ball rolling:

"Uh-huh."

"I see."

"Fascinating."

"Oh."[1]

The Road Map: Talk about How God Has Led You into Ministry

When you need a transition sentence to steer the conversation to talk about how God has led you, you might say, "When we talked by phone, I indicated that I wanted to bring you up-to-date on what the Lord has been doing in my life."

Talk about your spiritual journey. This could include going back to your salvation testimony, your involvement with a local church, your burden, or how the Lord has allowed you to use your spiritual gifts. It all depends how much the prospective donors already know about your story and how much they want to know. But talk specifically about the way God has called you into ministry.

Don't be lengthy, but share the instances that show God's leading in specific ways. Give illustrations and tell stories of God's faithfulness. In my case, the influence of my home and upbringing was significant. My family has been ministering in Chicago's inner city for more than ninety years. I would include that in my script.

After you finish this section, there should be no doubt in the prospect's mind that God has led you and that you need to fulfill His purposes. Include any or all of the following influences in your Christian experience in your script:

- Salvation decision
- Influence of home church
- Key Christians who have affected your life
- Christian books that have influenced you
- A crisis in your life

- Exposure to other full-time Christian workers
- Home influence

Place the influences in chronological order to help yourself rehearse your telling of the Lord's leading. Some refer to this as an explanation of the "Lord's call." Others who do not stress a special call to ministry will explain the events as a growing conviction from the Lord that they should undertake the work they have tackled.[2]

The Globe: Talk about Your Organization

Now that you have brought the person up to date on your life and on God's leading, your prospects need to become acquainted with the organization with which you will work. Discuss any of the following points:

- The vision of your organization
- Where they serve
- Whom they serve (information and statistics about the people served)
- Distinctives of your organization (What makes it unique?)
- Where you will minister
- The leadership of the organization
- When you will leave for your assignment
- What is happening in your target field

Talk about your commitment to the organization. Show your excitement. Talk about your compatibility with the mission's philosophy of ministry. Convey the assurance that you fully support the mission, its leadership, strategy, and policies. People need to see that you are not just venturing out on your own, that you are accountable. They want their money to be used faithfully in ways that count.

If your organization has a quality DVD, this could be a good place to use it. Although it cannot be shown during short, twenty-minute presentations, it can add a positive element to a longer appointment. On the other hand, it is not critical that you show it. You, your passion and excitement are far more important than all the technology out there. Another option is to leave a copy for prospective donors to view at a later time.

Literature about the organization could be helpful and can be left for later reading.

Literature about the organization could be helpful. If you have these materials, walk the prospective donor through them in a brief overview. You don't want prospects reading as you are giving your presentation. Materials can be left for reading at a later time.

The Glasses: Share Your Vision

It is vital that your supporters catch your vision. People don't give to meet a need; they give to support a vision!

Convey your burden with conviction.
Convey your burden with emotion.
Convey your burden with sincerity.
Convey your burden with confidence.

As you prepare your appointment script, it may help you articulate your vision to draft along these parameters:

1. Identify specific reasons why you joined your organization.
2. Describe the specific ministry to which you are assigned.
3. Explain why your personal ministry is important.
4. Describe what you want to achieve. Share goals that are realistic and measurable.

You might begin this way: "I firmly believe God has called me to serve with the ABC Organization. My job will be to _____. My vision is _____."

Several years ago, Sharon Murphy, one of our missionaries at ICI, put her vision this way: "My vision is to see these inner city girls saved, discipled, attend a Christian college, marry Christian young men, and establish Christian homes." Her vision has been realized. Two of the young girls from the inner city discipled by Sharon have attended Moody Bible Institute, where Sharon herself had attended. Today both of these young women are married and have wonderful Christian families.

If your vision is for children and the Lord has allowed you to work with children, then you might focus on one young person with whom you have worked in the past. Paint a word picture of how you affected that little one's life.

I will never forget the first day Juan came to our ministry. He was a tough Puerto Rican boy no older than nine. One night he didn't like the way things were going with the ministry. He grabbed some of his friends, walked down the three flights of stairs, picked up a rock, and put it right through my car window. I began to invest time with that tough boy, and he came to know the Lord. Now he goes to church with me and plans to go to Bible school.

Potential supporters want to be introduced to real people. Statistics alone will not impress them. So paint a picture to help them catch your burden for the lost. Display God's fingerprints all over the ministry. Whatever your dazzling vision may be, be enthusiastic and convey it to others.

After sharing your vision, seek a response by asking one of the following questions:

"Does this give you a better idea of what we will be doing?"

"Does this generate any questions on your part?"

"Do you see the value of what we will be doing?"

"Any comments?"

Write down your vision, take time to practice presenting it, tell it to a friend, and get it down pat. You will find that Baby Boomers, especially, want specifics. If they intend to donate $5,000 a year to your ministry, they want to know what that $5,000 will do. Tell them why you are going and what results you will see. Talk about the return on their investment. Be specific. Talk about ministry impact!

The Blueprint: Talk about Your Financial Plan

God has led you to affiliate with a Christian organization and has given you a vision. Now your potential donor must be made aware of what you need financially and how they can be involved. Remember it is more about giving them the opportunity to give than about you needing the funds.

To stop before sharing your need conveys the message that you don't need their help. However, as members of the body of Christ they need to be made aware of your financial needs so they can intelligently and prayerfully consider their role in meeting them.

You can introduce your financial need using these words: "The Christian organization I have been called by God to serve with has given me the responsibility of raising one hundred percent of my personal support. It is my job to seek friends committed to me and to my vision to help meet my support need."

At this point, ask your friend if he or she understands how the support system works. Some people have no idea that you must ask individuals to pledge toward your support. Ask, "Are you familiar with how individuals on support must raise their funds?" If they are not, give a more thorough explanation.

If necessary you could discuss the components that make up that support. I make it a practice of only providing information people request. So I might begin by stating the monthly amount required for my support. If they seem surprised by the amount or otherwise interested, I might break it down for them in this way:

My organization has asked me to raise the following:

Salary	$xxx
Insurance	$xxx
Administrative cost	$xxx
Retirement	$xxx
Projects	$xxx
Travel	$xxx
Start-up costs	$xxx

The total need per month is $xxx.

Now pause and ask if the prospective supporter has questions. That will give you an opportunity to hear what is going through his or her mind and handle queries or objections. It's important to deal with these at this point in the presentation. If you don't deal with them now, your prospective donor may sidestep your request for support later.

Most organizations will take a percentage for administrative costs that help cover some of the mission's overhead—costs to maintain the mission headquarters, secretaries, receptionists, training, and so on. Some donors do not understand or want to give money toward administrative costs. The way you respond is critical. Enthusiastically support your organization and its policy and be prepared to defend that policy. Without your organization's expertise, office assistance, and resources, you would be on your own. Although administrative costs don't cover your actual expenses, the organization's costs help keep you in your ministry.

Also, it would be wise here to explain your commitment to the individual donor. Campus Crusade for Christ identifies at least three commitments:

1. To serve faithfully.
2. To communicate regularly what God is doing through your ministry.

3. To share prayer concerns with one another.

Any ministry vision is obviously going to have a price tag. Donors and prospective donors know that, but they need to be reassured that as they give, there is a plan in place to see the vision fulfilled and realized and that you will keep them apprised of progress. Do your homework; be prepared for a lot of questions, especially if you are meeting with business professionals who think and operate with both the big picture and details. Get your ducks in a row! They will want to know your plan, feel assured that you are proactive, and understand that you have identified a group of key people you will meet with to ask for their financial investment. No one wants to be the sole supporter of your vision. Donors need to be reassured there is a team of financial supporters to take you across the finish line.

> *Donors have an important question in the back of their minds:* **Where do you want me to fit in?**

As you have presented your ministry and vision, your donors have had an important question growing in the back of their minds: *Where do you want me to fit in?* That brings you to the last section, where you will challenge the potential supporter in specific terms.

The Uniforms: Ask for Specific Help

If you have done your job well, it ought to be clear to your prospect that God is active in your life. You are a part of an exciting ministry, and you and the organization are faced with significant opportunities. There is one last question to be discussed—what can he or she do financially to help meet your vision? Here's where your team of supporters has its chance to grow.

You may give the best presentation of your life and answer all your prospect's questions, but the job still won't be done. You need to ask him or her directly to become one of your donors. If you have done your homework before the appointment, you will already have estimated an amount, or a range, you would like to challenge the donor to give.

The next question is the most critical of the entire visit. What you say and how you say it are vitally important. Even your body language has got to convey that you are about to deliver a very important message. Too many inexperienced fundraisers leave too little time at the end and then race through this final part of the presentation, leaving no time to prepare the prospect for the "ask."

Before you ask,

- slow down your pace,
- pause,
- make eye contact (to ensure the prospect is in receiving mode, locking into your message),
- put a smile on your face,
- speak with sincerity,
- be specific about what you are asking for, and
- speak with confidence and boldness.

If you're asking properly, your prospective donor should know for certain that (1) he is being asked a very important question, and (2) he needs to respond.

It's easy for a donor to respond when you have been clear and specific about what you are asking. State your request for financial support in terms of a specific pledged amount, or in a range of dollar amounts.

"The Ask"

Convey that you are about to deliver a very important message.

You might ask for a specific amount:

"To reach my goal of $_____, I am looking for individuals who will be able to invest in my ministry. Would you be one of those people who would support me at $_____ per month?" (Ask for a quarterly or annual gift, if that is the donor's preference.)

Or you might ask in a range:

"To reach my goal of $_____, I am looking for individuals who will be able to invest in my ministry. I am looking for people who could support me at, for example, $_____ to $_____ per month. Would you be one of those who would support me in the range of $_____ to $_____ per month?"

Wording is everything. Use words you are comfortable with yet will call for a response. Avoid vague or weak words, such as: "I am sure you probably have other places you are giving, but maybe you would think of helping me." Or, "Would you give this some thought?" You need your potential donor to make a decision, not just think about it!

Once you've made "the ask," then comes the power of the pause. Don't do what comes naturally! Your natural tendency will be to jump in to fill the dead silence that occurs while you wait for the donor's or prospect's response. If you jump in to rescue the prospect, you may inadvertently remove the "ask" from the table. Let your prospect reflect on your request and take full advantage of the power of the pause. Be quiet, and let the prospective donor take charge of his or her own response.

One good friend of our ministry was excited about our vision. I sat down with him, shared the vision, and proceeded to ask for a very sizable gift. Then I remained quiet and saw drops of sweat rolling down his face. I kept quiet. Finally, he broke the silence and said, "Yes, I believe the Lord would have me do that." I challenged high, and he responded.

Bring the Prospective Donor to a Point of Decision

When the prospect breaks the silence, you will hear one of four responses.

Response 1: *"Yes, I would be glad to support you at $xxx."*

Thank your supporter, showing your excitement and appreciation. Be sure to clarify the amount of the gift and the frequency.

Response 2: *"No, we are unable to support you at that level at this time."*

Begin by introducing a lower gift amount: "Would you feel comfortable with $75 [instead of $100]?" This gives the prospect an option, without dropping the amount significantly. For example, I wouldn't advise dropping from a request for $100 down to $25. Your somewhat reduced offer may relieve the prospect's feelings, especially if he really would like to support you but the suggested amount was simply too high.

If your prospect still feels uncomfortable with that amount, simply ask, "What would you feel comfortable in giving?" You do not want to engage in full-out negotiations—not at all! You simply want to leave the door open for this friend to give to your ministry in his own way.

You may sense that this prospect's issue is an inability to provide pledged support. That leaves the door open for a special gift. You might say, "Not only do I have to raise my monthly pledged support, but there are special needs that I have such as _____. You indicated that you feel you cannot make a pledge at this time. Would you make a special gift of $150?" Or, "Would you make a special gift in the range of $100 to $150?"

You'll notice I used the words *special gift*. I prefer not to say "one-time gift." The term *one-time gift* gives the impression that this is the last gift this donor will give. It's important for the donor not to feel "finished"—and even more important for *you* not to think you are finished.

Some givers do not want to be committed to a pledge but enjoy respond-ing as needs arise. They are spontaneous givers. These special-gift donors play a big role in your fundraising strategy. Ministries, organizations, and mis-sionaries will always have special projects that need funding. For example, a missionary going overseas might explain outgoing expenses. You already have listed on your script several projects or needs from which prospective donors can choose. It will help you discover what kinds of projects are of greatest interest to them.

You will be amazed at the number of special gifts that can be collected in this way. Also, recognize that if you do your job of thanking and loving those people, some will continue to give future special gifts, and some may even-tually become pledged donors. But the donor relationship begins with that initial visit when you ask for a gift.

Inner City Impact has numerous special gift donors. Every quarter I call one specific donor and give him an update. He asks for a letter and, like clockwork, several hundred dollars come back in the mail. I have learned his style and rhythm in giving.

Response 3: *"We need some time to review our commitments and pray about this matter. I don't believe we can give you an answer today."*
Begin by saying, "Can I answer any additional questions for you? Is there any further information you need from me?" Make sure you remove any obstacles and issues that may be holding back these prospects.

*Apply the
48-Hour Rule*

But a request for time to think and pray is valid, and indicates the time to apply my 48-Hour Rule. You want to give the prospects time to pray and review their giving, but you don't want a long time to pass because their excitement for your presentation can wane and other demands on their time and attention and resources may distract. Two days, or forty-eight hours, is a good time frame.

Remember, you want to move people to a point of decision. In this case, prepare for a follow-up call. If worded properly, you will have an open door to walk through when you make that call. You could use the following wording: "Today is (Tuesday). I will plan to call you on (Thursday)." Try to pin down a good time to call. "How about if I call between seven and nine Thursday evening?"

It is important that you control the follow-up call. You offer to make the call and then take responsibility for it. If you leave it in their court and they don't call back, it can be uncomfortable for you to follow up. Setting up the follow-up in this manner makes it a lot easier for you. For example, when you make the follow-up call you can say, "Bob, it was great being with you on (Tuesday). As we agreed, I am calling today (Thursday) to follow up our meeting. You'll recall I had challenged you to a gift of $100 per month. Can you do that, so I can see my ministry move forward?"

It helps to restate that amount. The prospects could have easily forgotten, or they might be thinking of a lower amount and you have a chance to pull up their vision.

If they need more time beyond the forty-eight-hour follow-up call recommended, I would just replay the forty-eight-hour rule. "Today is (Thursday), so I will call you on (Saturday)." There is no magic in the forty-eight hours. If they want to schedule the follow-up in three or four days, that is fine. The point is you need to know what your next step is.

Response 4: *"We cannot provide either a pledge or a special gift."*

Your prospects have done exactly what you wanted them to do: made a decision. Most no's fall into one of two categories.

In the first group, the prospects' body language or words signal, "I really like you. I believe in what you are doing. I wish I could help you, but I simply can't help at this time." If that is the case, ask, "When would be a good time in the future to get back in touch with you? When might your circumstances change?" I would add, "I do want to stay in touch with you."

In the second group, the prospects' body language or words send the signal, "You are not a high priority for me. I am not interested in your cause. You are wasting your time and mine." When you get that signal, graciously thank the prospects for their time and then make a decision whether you will keep them on your ministry's mailing list.

When someone says no, I initially feel discouraged and let down. But soon I remember that it is not a personal attack against me. The Lord will provide for my needs.

Because you are approaching people who know, trust, and care for you, then you will not get a lot of absolute no's. If you continue to work through your network of people, those who say no will not be the norm.

Handling Objections

It is possible a fifth response will appear: one of the objections outlined in chapter 12, pages 103–5. Instead of raising the objection before the meeting, the person raises it now. Look at the responses listed on those pages and you may be able to clarify a misunderstanding or a need for more information. In addition to those mentioned there, here are additional objections that may be addressed:

Objection: *"We have just had a financial setback."*
Response: "I am sorry to hear that. I certainly will remember you in prayer, and I will pray that the Lord will make it possible for you to participate at a later date. When should I plan to get back in contact with you?"

Objection: *"I can't say I have ever heard of your organization."*
Respond by identifying Christian leaders or pastors they know who speak highly of your organization. Also identify any associations or organizations with which your mission is affiliated that they might know about, such as ECFA (Evangelical Council on Financial Accountability).

Objection: *"My income fluctuates and I am not sure I can make a pledge."*
Response: "I understand. Is there a particular time of the year when you receive your income? Do you receive it quarterly, for example?"

The prospect may work on commissions or receive bonuses that are hard to predict.

Once you know the pattern, maintain contact with this prospective supporter. In case of a high-priority prospect, I would call two to three times throughout the year. When calling, I use these words: "I would like to keep in touch with you and give you updates on my ministry." Schedule a call on your calendar prior to their anticipated income arriving.

One man I know decides how much he will give each year once he knows the size of his bonus check. I know when that bonus check comes, but throughout the year I call and keep ICI in front of him. Every year Inner City Impact receives a good-sized check from him.

Objection: *"Well, what is the minimum pledge you are looking for?"*
Don't respond by giving any minimum dollar amount. Respond with the amount you had originally intended to ask. It is important to get people to raise their vision beyond the minimum. "I would love to be able to count

on a monthly gift of $xxx."

Anticipate Objections

What other objections do you anticipate? How will you respond to them? Take a minute to jot them down.

Eric Floreen, together with Missionary Aviation Fellowship of Canada, provides eight principles to remember when dealing with objections.[3]

1. **Listen** to the concern.
2. **Respond** to the concern. "I really appreciate the fact that you want to think it over and make a decision based on what the Lord wants you to do."
3. **Clarify.** "Just to help me clarify my understanding, what questions do you need to work out in your mind?"
4. **Allow** the potential donor to answer, listen carefully, and ask relevant questions. "In addition to that concern, are there any other reasons you would hesitate to join the team?"
5. **Thank** the person for clarifying his concerns. "I appreciate your openness. I am not here to pressure you into making a bad decision, but I would like to be able to give you enough information to make a good one."
6. **Answer** his concerns. "Does that fully answer your questions?"
7. **Re-explain** the need. "As I mentioned earlier, we are excited about what God is doing through our ministry. I am looking for the Lord to raise up a team. I sincerely believe that through an investment in my ministry, you can have a vital part in touching the lives of people."
8. **Ask** again. "I would love to have you on my team. Because of the urgent nature of my work, I would like to know as quickly as possible who will be involved in my ministry. Do you think I can count on you to be part of my prayer and financial support team?"

In summary, there are three points to remember in dealing with the uncommitted:

1. Clarify the concern.
2. Answer the concern.
3. Ask in principle.

Asking for Referrals

Ellis F. Goldstein, who is the director of Ministry Partner Development for Campus Crusade for Christ, provides some excellent advice on asking for referrals. Goldstein recommends following the ask with a request for referrals.[4]

This is wise, because excitement and emotional energy are building during the meeting, and then relaxes after the "ask." This is a perfect time to keep the ball rolling and get referrals. It would not be wise to do all the paperwork and then return to talk about referrals. Goldstein feels asking for referrals is the most significant part of the appointment. Your appointment is not over until you ask for referrals.

Asking for referrals may be the most significant part of the appointment.

Goldstein recommends always asking for referrals during a face-to-face appointment—and not by e-mail or over the phone, or by leaving a form for the donors to fill out. This request for referrals belongs in the context of a relationship. People are most excited about your vision right after they've heard your presentation. It's easier for them to say yes in person, and you have their undivided attention. If you choose to ask for referrals days after the appointment, you could find yourself caught playing phone tag.

Just as you've drafted all the points to cover in the appointment to this point, be sure to script your request for referrals ahead of time as well, practicing until you feel comfortable.

The Referral Script

After you've received a response to your request for support, Ellis suggests that you transition by saying, "There's another way that you can help." Immediately pull out paper and pen. That action shows your seriousness and your need to get their participation.[5]

A Positive Statement

Start with a positive, intentional statement. You might say, "I want to report to my ministry assignment as quickly as I can, but I don't know enough people to talk to about my ministry."

Introduction

"I have something I want to run by you. I was wondering if you'd be able to suggest a few friends I could introduce to my ministry." Your wording is critical. For example, don't ask if your donor knows others who might be "interested" in your ministry. "Interested" is too limiting.

Key Question

Ask the question that puts the donor in your shoes: "If you were going into full-time Christian work, who would you call to be a part of your support team?"

Without waiting for an answer, go on to the next question, "For instance, whom in your neighborhood would you talk to?"

You've done this before when you brainstormed your initial contact list. Help your donor think through his or her own network. Begin with a broad group, like contacts at church, and drill down, asking, Who in your Sunday school class? In your Bible study? In your small group? Serving with you on a committee?

Touch on family, business, social, and other networks that your donor is part of.

A broad question such as "Who do you know?" usually triggers no names. So help your donor through the process by suggesting specific categories.

Gather as many names as possible. All you are doing at this point is brainstorming, and no name is bad. Don't be surprised if your prospect or donor will stop and begin qualifying the names. This is normal. But don't take time to qualify the names. Also recognize that neither of you has enough information to make the decision on whether the person is going to give or not. Any decision you would make would be based on your feelings and not fact.

Be prepared to overcome reluctance.

For example, the prospect or donor might say, "I doubt if that person could be of help to you," or "I haven't talked to the person for a long time," or "That guy is out of work."

Keep your prospect focused on brainstorming names to give you. Remind the prospect that presenting your ministry is much more than just finances. You want to share what the Lord has been doing through your ministry.

Review the list.

Once you have the names listed, go through the list with the prospect, taking notes about the various people you've listed. You might ask:

What do they do for a living?

How long have you known them?

Do they have a heart for the Lord's work?

As you listen to the prospect's response, try to gauge which contacts your donor might consider high-priority prospects, those with a greater capacity to give and a heart for giving.

Follow up.

Beginning with the high-priority prospects, work your way down the list, asking your donor to help you connect with the contacts. Always aim at the ideal. In this case, the ideal would be the three of you meeting together.

Would you set up a meeting for the three of us to meet?

Would you set up a three-way phone call for us?

Would you make a call to introduce me, to be followed up by my call?

Would you send an e-mail or letter of introduction?

It is important that you contact referrals as quickly as possible because you don't want to be embarrassed when the donor comes back to you and asks, "By the way, how did your meeting go with Mr. and Mrs._____?'

You dare not overlook this part of the appointment. Sooner probably than later you will find yourself asking, "How do I find more contacts?" Every appointment gives you the opportunity to answer your own concern and question.

Some Housekeeping Matters

Before you leave your appointment, you need to establish the next steps. Some organizations have a commitment form that needs to be signed by the donor.

Find out how your donor wants to make the gift—by check, credit card, or electronic fund transfer. If they want to pay by check, ask them to provide the check right then. Otherwise, settle with the donors on the date when they will start their giving. If for some reason they don't start on that date, it is easy for you to follow up with a call when you have an agreed deadline.

Remind your donors that all checks should be written to your organization. Leave any response envelopes or documentation needed to streamline the process.

Closing the Visit

If your visit is with a busy professional, guard your time carefully. Stay within the time agreed upon. If you need more time, ask for permission to extend your meeting or consider rescheduling it. If your prospect is not pressured for time, consider spending more time. The more time you spend, the more you will help them feel a special part of your support team.

When you are ready to close your visit, this is an ideal time to get their commitment to pray for you. If you have a prayer card, that could be left. As you go, take away a note regarding ways you might pray for these donors.

Thank them for their time, and leave some literature. Then close by praying for them, their family, career, and the ministry the Lord has given you.

After the Visit

Immediately after the visit take a pad of paper, a digital recorder, or a laptop and record notes on the visit. If your spouse or a ministry partner is with you, one of you can record these things as you leave the appointment. If you are alone, you might pull to the side of the road and recall everything you can about your conversation. If you wait too long, you will forget vital details.

Record essential information about your donor, such as *the date of your visit, their spouse's name, children's names and ages, everyone's birthdays, their wedding anniversary, and hometown*. Other information can include their *hobbies, career(s), directions to their home or office, organizations to which they belong, names of other ministries they support, projects they like to support and projects they do not like to support*. If you know *their giving patterns*, i.e., when they give (monthly, quarterly, end of the year), and how much they give and how they give (through their church? Stock?), be sure to note that as well.

Of course, *list any prayer requests they have mentioned*. Other information you may have gathered during your time together might include *churches they have attended, and ways you can thank them* (readers might appreciate a Christian book). If they are a professional or owner of their own business, *include the name of their personal assistant or receptionist, and for business owners, their product, profit, and competition*. Finally, list any names of future prospects and mutual friends they may have mentioned.

Within twenty-four hours, follow up with a letter or e-mail thanking donors for the appointment and restating any commitment made. People will appreciate your promptness.

Role-Play a Visit

Once you've thoroughly scripted a possible appointment, and before the actual visit, a critical part of your training would be to role-play the visit. Ask a friend to critique your presentation.

Assign your friend the role of a real person you have pictured in your mind, to help set the stage for your friend and for you. Who is the prospect? His or her name? Their age? Career? When did you last see them?

This background will make it easier for your partner to play the role of the prospect. For yourself, also prepare ahead of time the dollar amount that you plan to use in the "ask."

Confidence comes from experience.

Remember, practice makes perfect. The more you perfect your presentation, the more relaxed you will become. Don't forget that confidence comes from experience.

Tips for More Effective Visits

If you find that few people are investing in your ministry, or that you are consistently receiving low pledge amounts, Mission Aviation Fellowship of Canada offers the following explanations for the problem and solutions for resolving the issues.[6]

LOW AREA: *Few people investing*

Possible cause	Presentation is unclear.
Solution	Pray for clarity, and practice your presentation.
Possible cause	Unenthusiastic presentation.
Solution	Pray for enthusiasm during your presentation.
Possible cause	Not asking for investments.
Solution	Follow the script and wait silently for the reply.

LOW AREA: *Low pledge amount—few pledges and more spiritual gifts*	
Possible cause	Not stating a definite amount, so people are giving minimally per month or small lump sum.
Solution	Say, "I'm looking for people to invest $25 or $30 or $35 per month."
Possible cause	Unclear in communicating that you are looking for monthly investments.
Solution	Clearly ask for monthly investments.

Try not to be intimidated by the details of your script and of the appointment process. Remember your six word pictures to get you through each meeting in the right order, and keep in mind that you are building relationships. Though it may seem daunting as you begin, you have exciting days ahead—days of experiencing the great joy of seeing others get excited about participating in your ministry.

The important task after each visit is to track your support, which you will learn to do in the next chapter.

CHAPTER 14

STEP 7:
Track Funds

People Raising is all about people, and building relationships with your donors involves more than just keeping names on a list. These supporters are individuals. Recording and tracking your support is critical. You will need to have some sort of donor roster. I recommend maintaining two rosters, each tracking a type of donor.

Pledged Donor Roster

Your first roster will track the giving of those donors who have committed to send in their support monthly, quarterly, or annually.

You need a system to tell you what support has been pledged, what has been paid, what is expected to come in, and with whom you need to follow up. Here are further categories of information you will want to record:

Name
Pledge amount
Frequency (monthly, quarterly, annually)
Date of pledge
Agreed starting date (If pledged amount does not arrive by this date, you
    will need to call the donor)
Actual starting date (the date their first pledged gift arrived. This is
    helpful for future reference and for resoliciting)
Actual amount by month

As you review the actual giving of each donor, you will notice five trends.

1. A donor is giving exactly what they promised.
2. A donor increased his or her pledge.
3. A donor stopped giving.
4. A donor decreased his or her giving.
5. A donor gave a special gift beyond his or her pledged gift.

When pledged donors are giving exactly what they promised, make sure they are thanked and not forgotten or neglected.

Every action on a donor's part requires an action on your part.

When pledged donors increase their support, thank them. The donor who is excited because he is giving more will be waiting for your response of gratitude. If the fundraiser fails to acknowledge that increase, he takes away the joy the donor has in giving more.

When a pledged donor stops giving or decreases the amount of his pledged gift, call that person to discover why. Let's stop a minute and speculate why donors might have stopped giving.

Lost a job
Health issues
Family issues
Lost in the mail
Forgot to send it in
Organization credited the gift to the wrong account

With a phone call, you will get the reason very shortly. Some of these issues, which reflect disappointment and needs in the donors' lives, will require you to move into ministry mode and minister to them. These donors need your prayers and understanding. Money becomes secondary and ministry to them primary.

When a pledged donor gives a special gift, try to discover what prompted the gift. If the donor gave an extra gift because he received an annual bonus, put a note in your fundraising diary to check in with that donor at bonus time next year.

Special-Gift Donor Roster

Your second roster will track those donors who, for one reason or another, cannot commit support on a regular basis but can give from time to time. These donors play a key role in your total fundraising.

Here are some of the things you will want to record:

Name
Amount
Date of initial gift
Dates of gifts (Many special-gift donors give multiple special gifts over the course of a year.)
Giving interest (Which projects or needs ignited giving? Go back to these same people when a similar need arises.)

Staying on Track with Donor Tracking

When you receive a first-time gift, contact the donor, thank him or her, and determine if the donor intends to be a pledged donor or a special-gift donor.

Never forget that the special-gift donor could become a pledged donor if you do a good job of thanking him, loving him, and keeping him informed.

Be careful also not to lose sight of your undecided and non-donors. Some of them can be cultivated and may eventually become part of your support team. Remember, your goal is to move prospects to a decision. So keep the names of undecided and non-donors in front of you, and follow up on them. If you don't, they will get lost in the shuffle.

Don't forget the free software recommended in chapter 10, where we covered cataloging your contacts. I've found TNT free software especially helpful (www.tntware.com).

Keeping detailed records keeps your focus on these donors as individuals. It's worth your time and effort. Caring for these donors brings us to the next chapter, one of my favorites. I sure don't want to be perceived as the fundraiser who gets the gift and becomes invisible, nowhere to be found. No, I want to show my appreciation to those God has permitted to be on my team.

CHAPTER 15

STEP 8:
Say Thank You

Part of my DNA is thanking people; it just comes naturally. I learned the courtesy of gratitude from my dad. My family has served Chicago's inner city for more than ninety years. On spring breaks as a young boy I would go down to my dad's office. One thing that stands out in my mind from those days is the countless hours my dad spent thanking people.

I want to say loud and clear that I want to see you *raise* the funds but also to *keep* the funds. If that is going to happen, you will need to regularly thank people.

Why do some raising funds have a difficult time establishing consistent givers?

Why do some donors never give a second gift?

Why do some donors drop their financial support?

Many answers can be found to these questions, but I am convinced that many donors stop giving because those raising funds fail to say thank you. You need to recognize that expressing appreciation is a crucial aspect of your ministry.

The apostle Paul had a thankful heart and often expressed his appreciation to fellow believers.

> I thank my God through Jesus Christ for all of you, because your faith is being reported all over the world. (Romans 1:8)

> I always thank God for you because of his grace given you in Christ Jesus. (1 Corinthians 1:4)

I thank my God every time I remember you. (Philippians 1:3)

Paul's heart of thankfulness led to another action on his part—prayer for fellow believers.

We always thank God, the Father of our Lord Jesus Christ, when we pray for you. (Colossians 1:3)

We always thank God for all of you, mentioning you in our prayers. (1 Thessalonians 1:2)

It is important to develop a thankful heart and express your thankfulness both to the Lord and to your donors. Saying thank you can make the difference between a one-time gift and a donor who grows in interest and commitment to you.

I remember meeting with a donor who decided to support several of our staff. When the staff members failed to say thank you, the donor asked,

"Didn't they get my gifts?"
"Didn't they need my gifts?"
"Didn't they appreciate my gifts?"

Hurt by the lack of appreciation, the donor did not want to be hurt again. He chose not to send future gifts to those staff members who had not learned the importance of those two words "thank you." However, I continue to thank that donor, and that donor continues to send thousands of dollars to our organization.

Say Thank You Immediately

Three principles have revolutionized my life. They are not complex, but the key is to apply them day in and day out.

1. Say thank you.
2. Say thank you immediately.
3. Say thank you immediately in writing.

It's hard to miss the emphasis on immediacy here. Be prompt. Don't procrastinate. Put yourself in the shoes of your donors. You know how exciting and fun it can feel to give a gift. Imagine how it feels, then, when a long period of time goes by before you hear anything from the person to whom you gave the gift. Obviously, you would be disappointed, and the initial excitement of giving would be long gone. Those could very well be the feelings of your donor waiting to receive your response.

If you handle the first gift from a new donor properly and the giver feels appreciated, that donor is more likely to send a second gift. Eventually new donors might increase their giving and introduce you to other potential donors.

The size of the gift may dictate your action. If a person sends a sizable gift, you should call immediately and thank him or her and follow up with a personal letter or, if appropriate, an e-mail.

What to Include in a Thank-You Letter

Every gift must be acknowledged by your organization with a receipt and thank-you letter. It's your job to add your personal thanks through e-mail or letter. You will want to:

Acknowledge the amount.
Say thank you.
Share a story or some results from your ministry.
Keep the letter short.
Be neat.
Be prompt.

The Role of E-mail

E-mail—and other speedy forms of communication like Twitter and Facebook or texting—can certainly speed the thanking process. E-mail is fast, and it can be personal, but it usually doesn't carry the same weight of thanks as a real, in-the-mail letter. Perhaps the inconvenience and increased formality of a real letter show the donor that you think thanking him or her is worth the extra time and effort. It's also personal for the donor to see your handwriting—in a signature and postscript, or in a handwritten note.

One advantage with e-mail is that an e-mailed thank you can easily be forwarded to others. For example, if you send an e-mail to the missions chairman of a supporting church, he or she can rapidly pass along your thanks to the entire committee.

The best advice is for you to know your donors. Respond in a way that will please the donors most, not by doing what is easiest for you.

Special Thanks

Especially say thank you when

- A pledged donor sends a special gift above and beyond his or her pledged support
- A special-gift donor begins to support you monthly
- A pledged donor or special donor upgrades their financial support

By maintaining the pledged-donor roster and the special-gift-donor roster (see chapter 14), you will note when a gift comes in and can respond immediately. If you fail to respond, it could be a sign that you are not sensitive to your donors.

Other occasions when a note of thanks should be sent include any time:

- Someone has entertained you either in his home or by taking you out to eat.
- A person has performed special services for you, such as assisting you with your taxes, calling a pastor to set up a meeting, or inviting a friend to see a presentation about your ministry.
- Someone sent a special birthday, anniversary, or baby gift.
- A person has provided special favors such as overnight housing, meeting arrangements, gifts of clothing, or food.

In essence, any time someone does something special for you, you should recognize that generosity and say thank you.

God has given you a special role in your ministry, and many of the Lord's servants are waiting to minister to you. But remember, givers need to be thanked and appreciated.

1. Say thank you.
2. Say thank you immediately.
3. Say thank you immediately in writing.

After moving into a new community I found myself in need of a dentist. At my first appointment, the dentist asked what I did for a living and I indicated I was in the ministry. That introduced quite a few questions on his part. As I left, he said simply, "I am sure insurance will handle part of the bill; don't you worry about any other charges. God bless you in your work."

I went home and remembered my three principles: 1. Say thank you. 2. Say thank you immediately. 3. Say thank you immediately in writing.

So I sent him a thank-you letter.

Over the next year, my wife and three children went to the same dentist. Again, there was no charge. After each of their visits, I said thank you, immediately, and in writing.

One day one of our Inner City young people had a tooth that was killing him. I called the dentist, and he kept his office open long enough to see him and, again, charged us nothing. I'm convinced that my saying two simple words—*thank you*—made the difference.

He had been appreciated, not taken for granted.

How to Say Thank You

First of all, you're not in competition to outdo or match your donor's giving. It is neither expected nor realistic. It is the thought that counts.

The most important way to say thank you is to say it verbally and in writing. But let me add that there are many other creative ways to express your appreciation. One key to thanking individual donors is to consider that individuality. What do you know about that donor? From observing your donors and remembering to listen, listen, listen, you will have picked up some strong clues.

Did one of your donors once mention she is a chocolate-lover—and how specific was she about her preferences? Does another have a unique collection, or a special taste in music? Do you know what favorite sports a donor follows, or a favorite team? Could you pick up a book on a subject you know interests that donor?

Check the details you've jotted down in your donor catalogue or diary. Is a particular restaurant, garden shop, or hobby store a donor's favorite? Does your donor have a favorite color, or a color they've used dominantly in their home décor, and could your gift of flowers match that preference?

Because your fundraising has cultivated a real relationship with your donors, you will pick up clues, and your mind will generate many more options.

For Example

If phrases of appreciation don't come easily for you, or don't glide right off your pen or your keyboard, check out this excellent list (next page), compiled by Wycliffe, of good ways to express thanks. Notice the word *you*. Keep that focus on your donor. Make donors feel they are truly part of your team.

You are a continual source of joy and encouragement to us as you faithfully pray and stand with us financially.

I wonder if you realize that you have been a partner with us for eight years now.

Each time your check comes we realize that your prayers back it up. That is such an encouragement.

The Lord overwhelms us with joy through your faithfulness to us.

As Paul said to his partners, your funds are a fragrant offering, a sacrifice acceptable and pleasing to God.

Your prayers and financial investment cause us to praise God for His goodness.

Each month when our statement of funds comes and we find your name listed there, we stop and thank the Lord for you.

Whenever the Lord uses us in some special way, we're reminded that you are also a part of it.

Your prayers make a difference in our lives and work. And, of course, your faithfulness in funding this ministry is so helpful and encouraging. I hope you know what a joy you are to us.

Without you and others standing with us, it wouldn't be possible for us to serve God in the task of helping fulfill the Great Commission.

Isn't it good to know that God is producing lasting fruit through our partnership?

In heaven you'll meet many dear people who have come to Christ partly because of our ministry together in helping get the Word to them.

You, through your prayers and finances, are the Lord's way of sowing His Word that brings living souls to Himself forever. All praise to the Lord.

Wonderful friends like you are a blessing from the Lord. When you are so good to us, my heart's reaction is to start looking for someone to whom I can be an answer to prayer also. Thank you and thank the Lord![1]

Three Donor Entitlements

We live in an age when people often think in terms of entitlement. Let's apply that to your donor. You might say that donors have three entitlements.

1. They have the right to know whether you received the money or gift.
2. They have the right to know whether you needed the money or gift.
3. They have the right to know whether the gift was appreciated.

If anyone needs to convey thanks it is the Christian worker, and we can learn from others who have expressed their thanks as above. Remember, appreciation isn't appreciation until it's expressed. Express it!

Fifteen Practical Ways to Say Thank You

I close this chapter with a few more practical ways to say thank you. Here's a fine list of ways to thank your donors. Get creative!

1. I never get tired of thanking you for your support.
2. When David commissioned Solomon to build the house of the Lord, the people rejoiced because they had offered willingly and made their offering to the Lord with a whole heart. I thank God for your willingness and wholeheartedness in giving.
3. It's a joy to serve God in this ministry with you.
4. I thought of the story of the widow in Luke 21 today and praised God that you also reach past your surplus to give to the Lord. Thanks for sharing it with me.
5. We rejoice that you faithfully supported us this year. That meant a lot to us.
6. I am filled with thanks to the Father as you help supply my needs and make this ministry possible.
7. We praise God that you "do not neglect doing good and sharing." We appreciate how you share with us your gifts unto Him.
8. Your giving is a ministry of His grace to us.
9. You are a continual source of joy and encouragement to us as you pray and give so faithfully.
10. We thank God for you and pray that the Lord will supply and multiply your seed for sowing and increase the harvest of your righteousness.
11. I am glad that the Lord brought you into my life and for your continued support.

12. The Lord overwhelms us with joy through your faithfulness to us.

13. We appreciate your friendship and partnership. We love you!

14. Your prayers and gifts often cause me to praise God for His goodness.

15. Each month you bring a smile to my face as I see your gift. His blessings to you.[2]

CHAPTER 16

STEP 9: Conduct a Phone Appointment

In earlier chapters I indicated that the best fundraising strategy is to visit people one-on-one. Though you should visit as many high-priority prospects as possible, sometimes a long-distance trip is out of the question. What should you do then?

Now is the time to use a combination of social media, e-mail, and letters to set up a phone appointment. Because this particular strategy requires less time and effort, you may be tempted to fall back on this strategy for those who live nearby. But don't take shortcuts. You need to meet one-on-one with as many of your high-priority prospects as possible.

So if a phone appointment is necessary because a face-to-face meeting is impossible, take a two-part approach:

1. Make contact using social media, e-mail, or letter.
2. Follow up with a phone appointment.

First Contact

Thanks to the Internet, you have many ways of connecting with your friends and contacts. I don't believe there is only one way to accomplish this, and I am sure even more Internet tools will soon come on the scene. The key is to consider the individual people on your contact list and determine the best way of communicating with those particular people. Some of them may be friends you already interact with through Facebook, Twitter, or texting. That would be the natural way for you to reach them regarding your phone appointment.

Simply share your excitement for your ministry assignment, that you would love to connect by phone, and indicate you will follow up with a call. Make sure your contacts understand that you want to call when they have a significant portion of time to give the conversation so you can catch up with each other.

Be careful not to send out messages to many supporters all at one time, promising a follow-up call. Your contacts will be expecting your call, and it might take you a long time to fulfill the promise. Send out two or three, make those phone appointments, and conduct those meetings before you send out another small batch of messages.

You may encounter the same delays or objections to phone appointments that you ran up against with setting up face-to-face appointments. So review step five (Chapter 12, "Make Appointments") to capitalize on pointers for getting the appointment and handling objections.

Phone Appointment

If you have Skype capability on your computer and your prospect also has Skype, do your best to make your appointment a Skype one, which combines two-way voice communication with visual. That would be a next-best option to meeting in person.

Why not make a Skype appointment?

Your Skype appointment or phone appointment will follow the same pattern and script as your in-person meetings. So review step 6 (Chapter 13, "Conducting the Visit"), depending on your memorized visual reminders of the six steps (album, map, globe, glasses, blueprint, uniforms). The six parts of your phone appointment are the same six you would use in person:

1. Bring the person up-to-date with your life.
2. Talk about how God has led you into ministry.
3. Talk about the organization.
4. Share your vision.
5. Explain your financial plan.
6. Ask for specific help.

Remember you could ask in a range.

"To reach my goal of $_____, I am looking for individuals who will be able to invest in my ministry. I am looking for people who could support me in the range of $_____ to $_____ per month. Would you be one of those people who would support me in the range of $_____ to $_____ per month?"

Or you could ask for a specific amount:

"To reach my goal of $_____, I am looking for individuals who will be able to invest in my ministry. Would you be one of those people who would support me at $_____ per month?"

You will almost certainly receive one of the four responses we covered in chapter 13:

Response 1: "Yes, I would be glad to support you at $xxx."

Response 2: "We are unable to support you at that level at this time."

Response 3: "We need some time to review our commitments and pray about this matter. I don't believe we can give you an answer today."

Response 4: "We cannot provide either a pledge or a special gift."

You will want to respond to each of these as covered in chapter 13:

Response 1: Thank the positively responding donor, showing your excitement and appreciation. Be sure to clarify the amount of the gift and the frequency.

Response 2: Introduce a lower amount or a special gift for the person who declines to pledge monthly support.

Response 3: To remove any obstacles to giving, offer to clarify any additional questions or provide more information. If the prospect still doesn't want to decide immediately, implement the 48-Hour Rule, setting a time-and-date appointment for you to call back to reiterate your "ask" in specific detail.

Response 4: If the prospect's no signals a willingness to help but inability to give support, ask for a future date when you can connect with the prospect again. If the prospect's no seems more definite, thank your prospect and decide whether or not you want to keep this person on your contact list.

Remember, since you are contacting people who know, trust, and care for you, you will probably not get many no answers. However your contacts respond, try not to take the disappointment personally, and remind yourself that it is the Lord's business to provide for your ministry needs.

You will want to follow up your prospect's giving decision with a request for referrals. Review the details in step 6 (chapter 13) regarding techniques for collecting this important contact information. Again, this is best done in person, but if a person-to-person appointment isn't possible, Skype or phone is your next-best option.

The Last Resort

If all else fails—it's impossible to meet with your key prospects one-on-one in person and a phone appointment is out of the question—then you might have to make your "ask" using a letter, e-mail, or social media. But again this is a last resort!

Do your best to keep the letter or e-mail conversational and personal. Keep it as short as you can while including the basic information you would include if you were meeting in person. Think album, road map, blueprint, a globe, glasses, and uniform with your name on it. Make your challenge specific, with a dollar amount or a range. Express your appreciation. If sending a letter, don't forget to sign it and add a handwritten postscript; keeping it personal is essential for building relationships. Include a date and time that you plan to telephone to follow up this "ask." And then follow through on that commitment to call.

Keep the content positive and specific. Don't, for instance, write about your deficit. Instead shape your request positively by describing real needs to which the reader can relate—medical expenses, auto expenses, special training expenses, and so on. Share your vision and passion. Remember, the giver needs to give far more than any cause needs to receive a gift. There never is a need to apologize for asking; you don't want to appear to be a beggar rather than a child of the King.

There is no question that phone appointments can work, but much depends on how you work this plan. It takes discipline, but your friends will be excited to hear your voice and equally excited to hear more about your plans for ministry.

As you work through the contact list you brainstormed at the beginning of your fundraising venture, you may be worrying about what happens when you reach the end of that list. Running out of contacts is a real concern, and the next chapter will address that.

CHAPTER 17

STEP 10:
Expand Your Contacts

For weeks, things might go very well. As you see the Lord meeting your needs, you may feel positive and upbeat. You might raise 10 percent of your fundraising goal, then 15 percent, 20, 25, and on to 50 percent. Finally, let's say, you'll reach 75 percent of your funds raised.

By the time you reach that 75 percent, you may find that you are hardly focusing on the amount pledged but are preoccupied with concern over the remaining 25 percent. You may ask yourself, *How long will it take to raise the rest? Will I ever reach my goal and be fully funded?*

Your concern may grow as you reach the end of your early list of contacts. It's easy to get discouraged when the prospects run out. But the truth is that very few fundraisers begin with all the contacts they actually need to raise support. Before you get stuck at a dead end, I encourage you to study three methods for collecting referrals.

Decades ago, there was primarily one method for raising funds. Fundraisers would go from church to church to church, in ever-widening circles from their own town, county, and state, to neighboring states, and so on. These time-consuming, expensive efforts usually resulted in minimal support.

A much-improved paradigm is the key principle I introduced at the beginning of the book:

People give to people.
People give to people they know.
People give to people they know and trust.

People give to people they know, trust, and care for.

This principle can be summed up in one word: relationships. The reason the old paradigm was so ineffective is that fundraisers were approaching churches with which they had no relationship. There has to be a better way to grow your circle of donors—and there is. Here are three proven methods that work:

1. Conduct a donor-sponsored small group.
2. Ask donors for referrals.
3. Utilize the key person concept.

Method 1: The Donor-Sponsored Small Group

Your goal of getting your ministry in front of new people is often met by extending your relationships with the help of your current donors. The donor-sponsored small group could take the form of a meal or a dessert time, and it could be in a home, a business or country club, a restaurant, or another venue. Your donor invites friends, and you present your ministry to them.

Several years ago I asked one of our donors to gather friends for a dessert time. I was excited about presenting the ministry of ICI. That night I met a young couple who became interested in our ministry. They made an initial gift to the ministry. Through the years they have made several significant gifts. Dessert times are well worth the effort to make new friends.

The Planning Process

Planning means answering the typical questions: Why? What? Where? When? Who? How? How much?

Why? The goal is to expose new people to your ministry.

What? You'll carve out at time for presenting your ministry and vision. There's no need to consider this small-group time a fundraiser. Your focus at this point is to make new contacts, those with whom you might later meet in one-on-one appointments to ask for funds. The point of the small group is to get your vision in front of more people. Remember, "Visibility = Opportunity." If your donor who is sponsoring the small-group time knows the meeting is not a fundraiser, he or she will be willing to invite their friends and more people will attend knowing they are not expected to give. Exposing others to your vision and ministry gives them an opportunity to follow God's prompting to give. My philosophy is to capture their hearts; those who love your work will support you in prayers and in finances. Even though the small-group setting is not the place for you to ask for a gift, the question nearly always comes up during your presentation, "How do you fund your ministry?" That gives you the platform to talk finance without asking for the gift.

The ask is far more effective in one-on-one appointments than it is in groups. The reason I rarely pose a group "ask" is that groups do not make decisions; individuals make decisions.

Avoid the group "ask."

Consider what might happen when you pose a financial request to an assembled group. Bob, seated toward your right, looks across the room and notices Sue. Bob says to himself, *If anyone can make a large gift, it is Sue.* Meanwhile Sue spots Bob and says to herself, *If anyone can make a large gift, it is Bob.* So everyone lowballs their offered support. It's much more effective to meet with Bob and Sue individually, get to know them a bit, and, at the appropriate time, challenge them personally and raise their vision and their gift.

Where? The small-group get-together could take place in the home of a donor, a club, a conference room at a donor's business, or a banquet room. Let the host make the choice of venue.

When? There is no prescribed right time—morning, noon, night, weekend, weekday. Let the donor host address this. There is no right or wrong answer, but there are a few don'ts.

1. Try not to schedule a time during a busy holiday season.
2. Don't schedule a time that will conflict with other special events, for example, a church concert.
3. Don't schedule it too early in the evening when people are still commuting from their offices.

Who? The best host for the small group is a trusted donor who knows, trusts, and cares for you. A donor is a person who has already partnered with you financially. Remember, the greater the involvement of a donor, the greater his commitment to you. An event like this can involve your donor in your ministry in a significant way. Also remember, high-priority donors tend to attract other high-priority donors.

How many? It's best to keep the group small and intimate. When a group gets too large, the personal touch is lost.

How? The details that follow will help both you and your host in your planning.

Role of the Host

Some details of the small group belong to your donor host. They include:

1. Set a date.
2. Provide a place.
3. Make the guest list; send invitations; follow up with a reminder to guests.
4. E-mail guest list to you.
5. Provide a dessert or refreshments.
6. Assist in setup.
7. Introduce you while providing an endorsement of you and your ministry.

Your Role

Your role as the fundraiser for your work is to:

1. Follow through with the host.
2. Discuss plans and format for the event with the host.
3. Review the guest list provided by the host.
4. Interact with the guests.
5. Make the presentation.
   a. Express appreciation to the host during the meeting.
   b. Share your testimony.
   c. Introduce your organization.
   d. Share your vision.
   e. Provide time for answering questions.
6. Assist host in cleanup.
7. Review the evening with the host.
8. Send thank you letters or e-mails.
9. Follow up with guests.

Other Tips

Several days before the event, ask the host or hostess to give you a complete guest list. Try to obtain the following information about each person attending: name, name of spouse, address, home phone, cell phone, office phone, occupations, church, and other background information.

Study the list so that you begin to get familiar with the names. If the host does not give you the list before the event, arrive early so you can study the list.

If the small-group event includes serving food, keep the menu simple, but let your host or hostess decide. If your hosts want to make the group a dinner party or simple refreshments, that's their choice.

Sample Schedule

Arrive forty-five minutes early to set up, talk with your host, and seek any last-minute advice they might have to offer. Go through the guest list once more.

If you are showing a DVD, plan in advance to have a screen or TV, an extension cord, and an outlet at hand. You should be relaxed as you greet people, not disorganized and hurried.

As guests arrive, position yourself near the front door and introduce yourself to each person. A warm smile and a friendly handshake will create a good first impression.

Your donor host should begin the evening when he or she feels comfortable. They might want to wait for certain key people to arrive before beginning.

The host should welcome the group, make opening comments, and give an endorsement of you and your ministry. People who are new to you will rely on their friend's endorsement. But be sensitive. Some people are more skilled and comfortable in leading a group than others. Ask the host to prepare his comments prayerfully and to enthusiastically endorse your ministry.

Begin your own presentation by thanking the host for his or her hospitality and the guests for coming. Then you make your presentation, expressing your vision and burden. Tell the story of one person impacted by your ministry, and paint a word picture of that person.

Provide a question-and-answer session.

Close your time together with thanks to the host once again and to the people for coming. Indicate to the guests that you will stay in touch with them. (You decide what that will look like later.) As you close, distribute literature from your ministry—a prayer card, DVD, or brochure.

Enjoy refreshments or dessert as planned

Talk with guests personally as they leave.

After everyone has left, help your host clean up and sincerely thank this donor for all that he or she has done. Before you leave, debrief with the host and ask what feedback he or she may have received from the guests. Take the guest list out and review it name by name. Ask which friends the host considers to be high-priority prospects.

Once you leave, record whatever information you can recall about each guest. If you have a portable, handheld digital recorder, record your information on the way home. The more you record, the more it could help you in the future. Below is a sample list of items you might be able to add to your notes about the guests:

Career(s)
Names of other ministries they support
Church they attend
Names of mutual friends
Organizations to which they belong
Hobbies
Hometown

Listen, listen, and listen. Then record or write down information.

Follow Up

Within twenty-four hours, send a personal letter or use social media to thank the host and each guest. Indicate you would like to stay in touch and that you will send them an update on your ministry from time to time. That is a nice touch that says, "I am putting you on my list."

Just as you did with prospects on your original prospect list, rank each guest and follow through as prescribed. The "H" prospect (high-priority) warrants a personal call to set up an appointment. You might follow up an "M" prospect (medium-priority) with a phone appointment, as described in step 9 (Chapter 16). "L" prospects (low-priority) might best be followed up through social media or mail.

Because the host has given you the names, addresses, and e-mail addresses of the guests, you can add these names to your list.

Bathe your planning in prayer, get an early start, and have fun as you build new relationships.

Commonly Asked Questions

Your donor host might have some questions for you, such as:

Q: Will you ask for money?

A: I tend not to ask for money but use the event to allow new contacts to meet me and connect with my passion and vision. But there is no set rule, and there are occasions when asking for funds would be appropriate.

Q: Whom do you specifically suggest I invite?

A: Anyone who would be excited to learn about what God is doing in and around the world, and those who are able to support God's work through prayer and finances. Your donor might build a guest list through church contacts (the directory, a Sunday school class, a Bible study, a care group, a committee, etc.), relatives, neighbors, colleagues at work, club and civic-group contacts, their Christmas list, or address book.

The Out-of-Town Donor-Sponsored Event

If you are participating in a small-group event with an out-of-town donor, ask your donor host to schedule the event in the early part of your visit in the area. That will allow you time for following up with appointments during the remainder of your visit. An extended weekend visit offers a good schedule for maximizing an out-of-town dessert event or other small group:

1. Saturday: Conduct the event.
2. Sunday: Be present in the church. If possible, take part in the service. Give a brief report or speak to a Sunday school class.
3. Sunday and Monday: Follow up with appointments.
4. Monday and Tuesday: Follow up with contact appointments.

When I look back at the growth of Inner City Impact's donor base, I see how God worked as He expanded our network. As you study the example below, recognize that originally I only knew Paul. Because he introduced me to John, I met the others who joined our support team.

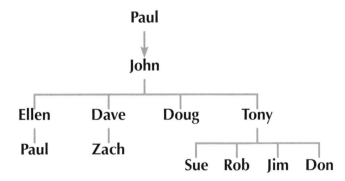

From Paul and especially John, an entire group of people caught the vision, one at a time. God can do the same thing in your ministry.

Method 2: Asking Donors for Referrals

The Lord has given you a network of friends who can introduce you to other people in their network. For this to work successfully, you must ask for your referrals from your friends who are already donors, who have bought into your vision and are investors. If you ask a friend who is *not* already a donor, consider what might happen. When your friend Mike tells friends about you, they will almost certainly ask, "By the way, are you supporting this ministry?" Even if your friend tells the referred friends what a neat person you are and what a great heart you have and how wonderful your ministry is, Mike's endorsement is actually worth very little. Why should Mike's friends support you if Mike isn't?

Perhaps you are already mentally identifying key donors who know you, trust you, and care for you. Whether they will help you further depends on how you have treated them. If they suffer from "donor neglect," they probably will not be eager to give you referrals. But if you've cared for them and encouraged them and brought them in to share your vision, they are much more likely to assist you. Those who are highly committed to you want you to be successful, and giving referrals is a way they can help.

We used the categories high-priority, medium-priority, and low-priority to catalogue prospects earlier in the fundraising process. The point was to reduce the time it takes to raise needed funds. In the same interest of saving precious time, my advice is for you to pursue referrals from your high-priority donors. If Linda is a high-priority donor who has committed $500 a month, guess what? Linda probably knows other friends who are capable of giving $500 a month. So begin by focusing on your high-priority donors.

Back in chapter 13, which covered all the aspects of step 6 (Conducting the Visit), I recommended that you ask for referrals, using a referral script based on the Campus Crusade format, beginning "There's another way that you can help." Review those steps on pp. 130–32, that include a positive statement about your ministry, a request to introduce your ministry to more people, use of a key question ("Who would you call to be part of your team if you were going into full-time Christian work?"), and your experience in brainstorming names, overcoming the donor's reluctance, reviewing the list, and followup, beginning with high-priority referrals.

Ask your committed donor to introduce you. Again, you should aim at the ideal, which would be a meeting with you, your donor, and the new contact.

If that is impossible, try a three-way phone call. If that, too, is impossible, fall back on an e-mail or letter of introduction. Then waste no time in making contact with the referrals your donor has so graciously provided. You don't want that donor to check in with you and find that you have disregarded his help and advice.

Method 3: Utilizing a Key Person

The key person is usually a successful professional in a community other than your own whom you ask to act on your behalf in raising your support. Sometimes it's effective to choose an older Christian, who has retired.

Campus Crusade offers the following pointers on how this key person might help you raise funds and how you might choose the best person for the job.[1]

Benefits of Using a Key Person

Consider how time-saving it could be to have an advocate at work before you arrive in another community, presenting your ministry and eliminating conflicts, and making appointments in that part of the world. Your key person will have established relationships in his community and can open doors and secure appointments that you might not be able to make.

Relying on a local key person decreases your cost of long-distance support development as he makes the phone calls and handles activities locally.

As you train your key person, you can pour your enthusiasm and training into him and then ask him to select someone else he could bring along to assist him, thereby giving you two key people in a given area.

Your key person is going to reap a great benefit as well—his own spiritual growth. As this friend prays, plans, and works with you, his faith will increase and his relationship with Christ will be strengthened. He will play a direct role in reaching people for Christ as he helps you develop support for your ministry.

Choosing the Key Person

Who is a person greatly interested in your ministry and who would help you develop your support? Check the list of professional people who have known you in the past and who would give time to help you. Pray, and be receptive to a name God might impress on your mind.

How Your Key Person Will Help

Your key person will learn all about you and your work as you brief him or her thoroughly (1) on the ministry of your mission, (2) on your personal testimony, and (3) on your purpose and ministry.

Your key person will help you in these specific ways:

1. Support you financially.
2. Pray for you daily.
3. Provide referrals.
4. Write letters of introduction.
5. Call for appointments.
6. Go with you to appointments.
7. Set up group meetings.
8. Sponsor a dessert time or home meeting.
9. Follow up some of your contacts during the year.

Remember, you will always be looking for people to add to your list. The Lord has people out there, but He depends on you to go out and find them. These three tools can put you on the right track. I trust this chapter has given you hope. You will be amazed at the number of new people God wants to bring to your team. It has been a long journey, but step 12 is just around the corner.

CHAPTER 18

STEP 11:
Cultivate Your Donors

Your goal is not just to get your funds, but also to keep those funds. For this reason, it is critical for you to keep cultivating your current donors. Maintaining and developing these donor relationships is not an option but a must.

Support cultivation is comparable to a farmer cultivating his field. He doesn't throw seed on the field and then leave it there. He prepares the ground, plants, fertilizes, waters, and weeds. As a result of hours of hard work, the farmer expects a good crop.[1] A fundraiser, too, must work his field by staying close to those who are currently supporting him to keep them on his team.

The missionary who doesn't cultivate his or her support may use many excuses:[2]

"I hate to write letters."

"I'm not the thank-you type."

"People don't expect personal notes."

"I'm too busy."

"I don't care."

"I cannot write good letters."

If you neglect your donors,

- They will find another place to invest—out of sight, out of mind.
- They will not consider your ministry a priority. If it were a priority, wouldn't you communicate that to them?
- Their commitment to you will decrease. They may not actually drop

163

your support, but they will remain less than totally involved.

- They will not be as willing to give you referrals. They will not want you to treat their friends the way you treat them.

Out of every one hundred individuals who stop supporting you:

- Four move away or die.
- Fifteen have made a decision that another organization can serve them better.
- Another fifteen are unhappy with your organization (and are telling others that).
- Sixty-six think you don't care about them.[3]

If your ministry is out of sight, it will be out of people's minds.

There isn't much you can do about donors who move or die, or even about those who have become dissatisfied with giving to your organization. But that 66 percent represents a great number of donors, and you can do something about the problem of donors thinking you don't care. This is really the only area that is remotely under your control.

"You cannot abuse people and expect them to help you," says Steve Rentz of Campus Crusade. He goes on to say that cultivation is not merely sending prayer letters to inform your ministry partners of your activities. It entails more than simply "reporting in" on monthly news or prayer requests. "Cultivation is the process of developing and communicating warmth and concern for your people. This involves a commitment to build relationships with your ministry partners just as you would build relationships with those in your field of ministry."[4] Support cultivation is ministry, and you should view your donors as part of a team, as your ministry partners.

The Bible regularly exhorts believers to thank God for all things. "It is a Christ-like characteristic to be thankful to God and people."[5]

With my mouth I will greatly extol the Lord; in the great throng I will praise him. (Psalm 109:30)

I have not stopped giving thanks for you, remembering you in my prayers. (Ephesians 1:16)

Let the peace of Christ rule in your hearts, since as members of one body you were called to peace. And be thankful. (Colossians 3:15)

Support cultivation is a process, a lifetime ministry. Your goal should be to develop relationships that will keep people on your team.

> *Develop relationships that will keep people on your team.*

Caring for Donors

Your perspective on the importance of donor care plays a critical role in how you'll handle this important aspect of fundraising. One mission organization offers this outline to contrast the negative and positive attitudes and steps regarding caring for your donors.[6]

1. Incorrect attitudes
  a. Viewing the support team as an inconvenience or added responsibility that consumes your time
  b. Desiring to get by as inexpensively as possible
     1) Not corresponding regularly because of the cost of postage
     2) Using inferior paper for prayer letters
     3) Thinking that small gifts aren't practical
  c. Assuming your support team is not concerned about you
  d. Seeing your support team only in a financial perspective

2. Correct attitudes
  a. Viewing team members as friends rather than as financial investors
  b. Depending on the character of God, realizing that He, the faithful One, provides for our financial support
  c. Endeavoring to be open and personal with your team
  d. Seeking to be generous with your time and money to cultivate your support team

3. Steps
  a. Pray for your partners—outline an organized way to pray for your support team. Decide how you will share prayer requests and answers with one another. Ask about answers the next time you see/talk to them.
  b. Communicate love. Help others feel needed, appreciated, and part of what you're doing. Minister to spiritual needs, helping them walk with God, understand His Word, and learn His will for their lives.
  c. Communicate regularly—set up a communication calendar/plan.

d. Maintain a personal communication record.

e. Maintain a year-end investment record.

f. Develop an information file on your supporters. It is an ongoing process.

g. Don't overlook children and other family members. Maintain a family network.

Communicating with Donors

How can you build a bond with your donors? By connecting with them in every way possible. What is the most effective way to maintain communication? Remember how the Harvard study ranked the effectiveness of communication? By far the most effective tools were the personal ones, with one-on-one contact the most effective. As personal as possible is a good rule of thumb as you work in practical ways to cultivate your support.

Visit Key Donors

As often as practical, meet with donors one-on-one. I set appointments regularly to have meals with donors, which is a very good use of my time and theirs. When one-on-one isn't practical, get together with groups of your donors who live in a given geographical area, with one donor serving as your host and inviting several others over for an evening.

Voice Contact

Phoning is one of the most practical and productive means of communication, and using Skype is a terrific way to stay in touch. There's a reason telephoning used to be called "person to person." Hearing another person's voice (and, with Skype, seeing his or her facial expressions as well!) still provides a strong connection.

Personal Letter

Beyond your regular monthly prayer letter, your readers will enjoy hearing from you personally. Ideally, the letter should be a down-to-earth, personal, handwritten letter. Sometimes I find the time for this while traveling. I've heard that author and speaker Josh McDowell has been known even to use the napkins on the airplane to jot notes to his supporters.

Second-best is the personal letter or note you've typed. This could be sent through ordinary mail or possibly as an e-mail.

Mass Letter or Prayer Letter

Discipline yourself to send a prayer letter on a regular basis. Some of these will be transmitted via e-mail, but for those letters that are actually printed on paper before mailing add a personal handwritten note at the bottom of the prayer letter.

I would rather see you communicate on a regular monthly basis with a straightforward prayer letter than a fancy, complicated newsletter that requires an immense amount of time and money to produce and is sent less often. The point is to keep open the lines of communication.

Jot notes in your daily diary to help you capture and remember what you want to communicate in the monthly letter. Plan ahead, and remember the prayer letter is not to ask for money but to keep interested people informed.

Your regular prayer letter will:

- Educate donors
- Deepen your relationship with them
- Enable them to pray intelligently for you; they need to be informed about answers to prayer as well as needs
- Maintain accountability; you need people to answer to
- Increase your partnership
- Keep your work in front of your donors, to combat the "out of sight, out of mind" syndrome
- Provide a feeling of ownership; donors need to feel part of your team
- Keep them informed[7]

Newsletter

Nothing excites donors more than to hear that your ministry is yielding solid results. They figure their investment is worthwhile if your ministry is accomplishing what you told them it would accomplish. A well-written newsletter helps communicate that. It differs from your prayer letter in that it has a more polished, jazzy, mini-magazine-type format. A newsletter can have headlines and short articles, a logo, and special column names, such as Prayer Corner, Family News, or Village Happenings. The point is to minister to your audience, bringing them closer to the Lord, express your appreciation for them, and stimulate donors with your vision.[8]

Let your imagination run wild. Use borders, graphics, photos, and varied type fonts to add interest. You can give your newsletter a name with a logo or masthead. Many missionaries personalize their newsletters using their family names, as in "The Bohm Bulletin Board" or "Prettos Progress."[9]

Of course if you have an actual graphic designer on your ministry team, you might be able to provide a professional look for your newsletter. But here are some questions for evaluating your newsletter's attractiveness and effectiveness.

Are paragraphs short?

Did you indent paragraphs (not block style)?

Did you make use of white space?

Are the grammar and spelling correct?

Did you use the active voice?

Did you use "you," not "I"? For example, "You would have enjoyed seeing . . ."

Did you use black ink?

Did you include charts, diagrams, or pictures?

Did you use dashes occasionally?

Keep the overall visual appearance appealing. CAPITAL LETTERS ARE HARD TO READ AND GIVE THE FEELING OF SHOUTING! Use of italics for emphasis is more effective.

Although you want to establish a definite layout, look for ways to vary the format and design. Use different textures and materials, pictures, graphs, and drawings.

Create a feeling of warmth in a newsletter. Catch the reader's attention by using good lead-in sentences. Talk about real people in a "you and me" style. Link paragraphs with connections: *of course, however, you know, now, so you see.* Keep to your point without long paragraphs. Express appreciation.

Develop a system for creating your newsletter. Be creative and use variety. Work on your writing skills. Develop a file of ideas.

Newsletters can be costly in terms of time. In terms of communication, a newsletter is less effective than personal and prayer letters. Your goal is to communicate your love and appreciation to your donors and to give them the satisfaction that they are helping you make a difference in changing the world for Christ. You are not competing to see who has the most dramatic newsletter.

Social Media

The Internet offers many ways to stay in touch with donors. But keep in mind how rapidly new technologies appear, and how users tend to fall in love with

the latest and greatest ways to communicate. It may pose challenges for you to operate in several applications of social media. And remember: using social media is not the best way to
raise funds; the best way will always be one-on-one, in person.
But the social media offer great tools for cultivating and staying in contact with your donors. Let's take a look at some Internet websites and their benefits and shortcomings. Recognize this is just a
sampling, and new ones are on their way almost every time you turn around.

Communicate your love and appreciation to your donors.

With millions of active users, Facebook (www.facebook.com) is a popular
way that people keep up with their friends. For fundraising purposes, you
might use Facebook to find old friends and connect with new ones, learn more
about the daily details of your contacts' lives, pass along information (including links to giving information or your organization's website, etc.). Facebook
even allows you to segment your list; for example, you could distinguish
between donors and prospects. A similar tool is LinkedIn (www.linkedin.com),
a social network linking business professionals.

That phone in your hand is another tool for growing relationships. Texting
is good for immediately sharing prayer requests, videos, or photos.

Twitter (www.twitter.com) offers many of the same benefits as Facebook
and is an especially good way to update others on your ministry or to follow the updates of your donors' pastimes. Twitter's specialty is the minute-
by-minute update, which gets delivered straight to your donors' cell phones,
if they have Twitter. Twitter may not be worth the investment of your time
unless you are going to use it regularly. There are limits to the amount of
text that can be sent at one time, and "Tweets" are being filtered by Twitter's
verifying process.

You may find it worthwhile to create a personal blog or a personal web
page. Your donors can check your blog or web page to see what's happening
in your ministry as you post new information day by day, almost like journal-
ing. Prayer requests, video clips, and photos can enliven your blog or web
page, both of which easily link with Facebook.

On YouTube (www.youtube.com), you might post a video clip presenting
your ministry. It's another way to bring sight and sound into the mix, making
your vision come to life for donors who can't visit your work in person.

For donors you can't easily reach in person, Skyping via computers is
almost the next-best thing. It's also a way you can provide audio and video for

donors who can't make it in person to an event or presentation. Skype turns your computer into a video phone and links with donors whose computers have a built-in camera.

E-mail has revolutionized contemporary communication, and there are marketing applications, such as Constant Contact, that can help you organize your donor list for sending large group e-mails.

High-tech allows you to be high-touch. High-tech (the Internet, your cell phone) allows you to be high-touch (in consistent contact) with donors. Every tool that can help you build that relationship is useful for People Raising.

Adding Value

Professionals who work in sales understand the concept of "added value." Basically, once a product has been sold, the transaction is over; the commodity changes hands, and payment is made. But good salespeople add something to the value already traded. They know that their extra effort will build a relationship with that client. The value they add could be as simple as conveying personal interest. For example, a realtor might phone or drop by several days after closing on a home to ask how the new homeowner is settling in. The person who sells a photocopier may, after the sale, include some copier supplies at no charge. The point is that the extra is unexpected and unrequested; it is a value added to the sale.

Your support team has expectations. They are interested in—and entitled to—information about your ministry. Some of those expectations are tied into their reasons for giving. In addition, they expect prayer letters, personal visits, reports, and so on. Every contact you make with a supporter bonds them to you and your ministry and increases their interest in you.

When you take an "extra-mile" step or give a tangible gift to a supporter, the results may be quite unexpected. Of course you do not give a gift for the purpose of receiving something in return; you give it because you love and appreciate your supporting team member. But your gift could generate prayer. It may generate more financial support. It could be the "gentle" nudge the Lord uses to propel another worker to the field. If nothing else, the gift will increase the sense of family and teamwork you are trying to generate.

Here's an idea bank for you to draw from in coming up with personal and creative ways to connect with your donors.

- Invite donors to the church or home at which you speak.
- Send updated family pictures.
- When reading an article that may be of interest to a donor, cut it out or make a copy to send to him.

> *A gift will increase the sense of family and teamwork you are trying to generate.*

- Send care packages with local food products.
- Call, visit, or send a card to a donor who is sick or in the hospital.
- Send a card for a donor's birthday and anniversary.
- Send postcards and greeting cards. Consider sending cards for holidays when people don't receive many cards (Thanksgiving, Valentine's Day, and July 4). Send your annual greeting card at Thanksgiving with special thanks to them.
- Major supporters should receive a tangible token of appreciation annually. Christmas is an excellent time to send a gift—something unique from your field of ministry perhaps, or an item that will stimulate a donor's spiritual growth or prayer life.
- Send special gifts—jelly, honey, books. When you give a book, try to meet a specific need, and write a note in the flyleaf.
- Send CDs or DVDs: musical, praise, sermon, updates of your ministry. You might even walk donors through a day in your ministry—hear sounds of the country, local music, and so on.
- Add to a supporter's collection of stamps, postcards, or knickknacks.
- Send small gifts from the field. Bring special gifts when home on leave. They don't have to be expensive—be creative.
- Entertain while on home leave.
- Get to know supporters' children. Remember that a gift (i.e., Christmas tree ornaments, pictures, small games) for a supporter's child goes a long way in deepening a relationship.
- Link pen pals between children in your local ministry and supporters' children.
- Provide information to supporters' children for school projects.
- Be a Vacation Bible School visiting missionary.
- Set up a telephone call to the church during worship service.
- Send recipes or crafts from the field.

I can't count the number of times I have heard pastors and mission committee members indicate they have not heard from a missionary in months or even years. In most cases, the church has done its part, but the missionaries have chosen not to keep the communication lines open. When that happens, not only does the missionary eventually lose his support, but he has robbed individuals or churches of the satisfaction of knowing what their gifts and prayers are accomplishing.

So stay on the lookout for additional ways to strengthen the bond between you and your supporters.

Involve your ministry partners in your work, and encourage participation initiated by them toward you. When a donor invests his time and attention in your ministry, he develops a deep sense of ownership—the ministry belongs to him, too. Here is a great list of ways donors can be involved in your work.[10]

- Pray for you.
- Phone you periodically.
- Accompany you on fundraising travel to develop friendship and help present the ministry.
- Host a home meeting.
- Type/mail your prayer letter—computerize the mailing list and print address labels.
- Give logistical help for home leave—locate housing, car, schooling, and so on.
- Pick you up or drop you off at the airport.
- Help you get settled or help prepare the home/garden for use.
- Give you a gift certificate for a special treat.
- Bring you up-to-date on "what's in and what's out" since you've been away.
- Host a party in your honor and spend time praising God for His work through you.
- Be sensitive to the length of time you need for cultural adjustments, if you're returning from international ministry.
- Help your kids "fit" back into local culture while on home leave.
- Babysit for your children.
- Help run errands.
- Provide occasional meals at transition times.
- Plan a ministry shower. Give a food shower.

- Send you off for a weekend of rest.
- Develop communication with your older parents.
- Provide money management/financial advice with power of attorney.
- Print the prayer card, business card, prayer letter.
- Provide feedback for your presentation.
- Help produce a PowerPoint or video presentation.
- Purchase clothes for your family.
- Build crates, pack barrels, provide trucking, give storage space, or help move.
- Send a video of key North American programs/sports if you are out of the area.
- Pack a birthday package/special care package, especially sending you items not available in your area.
- Send church bulletins and sermon CDs, church directories.
- Send a subscription to a newspaper or articles on trends.
- Provide a gift subscription to key magazines.
- Compile a list of services and supplies needed by you.
- Invite the supporting church to send a summer or short-term team to your area.
- Send books.
- Pre-address envelopes/aerograms for church members to write to you.
- Send party decorations and napkins for birthday parties.
- Encourage you during the emotional ups and downs.
- Learn what makes you feel supported and then do it.
- Visit. Write frequent letters. Send holiday cards.
- Write to your kids individually.

Your donors become real partners in your ministry in these tangible expressions of your growing relationship. It's closeness that will keep people on your team. Below is a real-life illustration of the principle of closeness.

Car salesman Joe Girard understands "closeness," and that understanding helped him sell more new cars and trucks each year, for eleven years running, than any other human being. In a typical year, Joe sold more than twice as many units as the salesperson who took second place. The secret to Joe's success was the added value of personal connection. He never forgot his customers, and never let them forget him either! Every month throughout the year they received a letter from him in a plain envelope, always a different size or color. "It doesn't look like junk mail you throw out before it is opened," Joe confides. The front of each card reads, "I like you." Inside it says "Happy New Year from Joe Girard" or "Happy George Washington's Birthday" or "Happy St. Patrick's Day."

Joe's customers love receiving the cards. Joe boasts, "You should hear the comments I get on them." Joe's cards would be just another sales gimmick, except that Joe genuinely seems to care! Joe has cared about every customer as an individual. He doesn't think statistically but emphasizes that he has sold vehicles "one at a time, face-to-face, belly-to-belly. Customers are not an interruption or pain in the neck. They are my bread and butter."[11]

Joe understands cultivating supporters. He sees them as people and thinks about their feelings and needs.

You will continue to care for the donors you've got, and resolicitation will be an aspect of that ongoing relationship in your fundraising program. The next chapter will show you how to resolicit donors.

CHAPTER 19

STEP 12:
Resolicit for Funds

You can always be raising funds by resoliciting current donors because there are donors on your list who need to be asked again. They have given, and you have maintained contact. They believe in what you are doing. It's possible that they may want to and may be able to give more. These are the folks that need to be resolicited.

Just as you may lose donors who encounter financial difficulties, you will also have donors whose financial picture is prospering. The financial status of a person can change for the better. A donor who began supporting you when he had children in college may have more ability to give if his children have graduated. A donor may have a new job or may have received a promotion. Such donors are in a position to increase their support.

It is much easier to get more money from an existing donor than to recruit a new donor. It is also more cost-effective and time-efficient. Challenging people in their giving is a crucial aspect of your fundraising plan. Resoliciting is a chance to challenge high.

Three Groups of Givers

As you gear up for a season of resoliciting, you will break your list of prospects and donors into three groups. The first group is your pledged donors, those who have committed to give to you regularly. You have their vote of confidence. This is a natural starting point for resoliciting funds. Your second group are those special-gift donors who obviously like you and your ministry but are not as committed as your pledged donors. The third group is made up of your non-donors, those you've approached in the past but who decided not to support you for one reason or another. Right now they are non-donors, but many may maintain an interest in you and your ministry. Resoliciting is an opportunity to pursue them once again. You will know which of your non-donors are people who are clearly decided against supporting your ministry, but there are probably some in this group who can be asked again at the right time.

The graphic on this page shows the three main categories: pledged donor, special-gift donor, and non-donor. Let's take a look, then, at how we will approach these three.

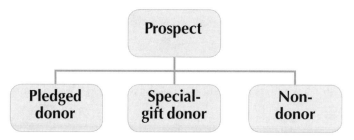

Pledged Donors

Your pledged donors are your real base of support. Regardless of whether they pledge monthly, quarterly, or annually, they should be challenged once a year to upgrade their giving. In preparing to resolicit these donors, remember that you are seeking to bring each person to a point of maximum participation.

Be prepared to make resoliciting these already-pledged donors a two-step process if necessary. Your first step is to ask them to increase their regular support. If a person currently supports you at $100 per month, you could, for example, ask him to increase his pledge by $50 per month. If a person currently gives $150 a month, you might ask for a $75 a month increase. If the donor is unable to take on these numbers, you might ask what amount of increase he or she feels comfortable in giving. There is no right or wrong way to suggest an increase. Be careful that you do not aim too low.

If they are reluctant or unable to increase their pledge, move on to step 2. Ask if, instead, they would be willing to provide a special gift. Identify specific special needs your ministry currently faces. If your pledged donor is willing to give a bit extra in this way, you are still coming away from the meeting with a financial gift.

Special-Gift Donors

Special-gift donors are a significant group of people who do not give monthly, quarterly, or annually with a pledge. Instead they help with special gifts. You can approach these givers with a different two-step process.

The first step is to encourage them to become pledged donors. If they are not ready to commit to regular giving, the second step is to secure another special gift. Giving for specific needs is the preferred style of giving for some of your supporters. You can resolicit this group three or four times a year as emergencies or unique projects (such as birth of a baby, need for a vehicle, training expenses) arise.

The Non-Donor

In working with the non-donor, recognize that a no is never forever. Last year when you asked these prospects for support, they said no. Since circumstances change, you can approach them again.

As you did the first time you approached these contacts, begin by asking for a pledged gift, and then follow up by asking for a special gift if they are not able to commit to regular giving.

Of course, you will have to use your judgment about how many times you will approach a contact before you decide not to resolicit from that source and go on to purge that name from your list.

Five Kinds of Donors

I am very confident if you follow this strategy for resoliciting, you will experience an increase in giving. Remember that it is easier, more cost-effective, and more time-efficient to get more money from an existing donor than to recruit a new one.

As you work with your donors, remember that donors come in all shapes, sizes, and temperaments. Here are five different types of donors.

Starters like to start a project. They catch the vision quickly and want to be with you from the beginning.

Finishers like the satisfaction of knowing their gifts pushed you over the top.

Project-oriented donors don't get excited about paying the utilities and rent, but they are turned on by special projects.

Impulsive donors respond quickly and gladly when presented with an urgent challenge.

Programmed donors figure out their giving for the year on January 1 and lock it in no matter how urgent or important your mission may be. Reach these givers in mid-December to ask for a commitment for the coming year.

It's important to keep notes on each donor and to know whether he or she likes to give regularly, to special projects, to emergencies, or in other giving patterns. Does he make a decision the first of the year? On a quarterly basis? When? Be there when he may be ready to give.

You've come a long way, all the way through the twelve steps of fundraising—beginning with your home church and getting all the way to resoliciting your donors. Where do you go from here? Read on.

IMPLEMENTING
your
FUNDRAISING PLAN

CHAPTER 20

Mastering the Six Critical Skills

Fast Forward

So we don't lose sight of the whole People Raising strategy, let's take some time to review the flow.

First we talked about cultivating a positive attitude toward fundraising and *the benefits of raising funds*. Next we explored *the biblical basis for raising funds*. We established that *it is okay to ask for funds*. The end of that session was the challenge: What are you waiting for? Go for it!

We *confronted the fear factor*. People Raising strategies help reduce the fear but never eliminate it. The Lord is with you, and it's His ministry. Fundraising *is really not about you*. You are giving God's people an opportunity to invest and partner in God's eternal program. Your donors have a greater need to give than you have to receive. Your donors might need you more than you need them.

We discovered that *the number one enemy of fundraising* is you. We saw the cycle produced by negative thinking, which can cripple your fundraising efforts.

You then got practical, exploring critical fundraising skills. You learned to *develop a fundraising* strategy built around two key principles: the principle of relationships (people give to people they know, trust, and care for) and the principle of contacting people you know in the most personal and practical way possible. You learned to *begin with your home church*, discovering the decision makers regarding funding your ministry.

You discovered how to *determine to whom you will go for funds*, keeping in mind that looking for prospective supporters is an ongoing process, not a one-time function. You learned how to take that initial contact list and *re-cord, catalogue, and prioritize your prospects,* keeping track of details, sorting your prospects as they move into donor categories, and prioritizing for a top-ten list as a focal point.

You were then ready to *get the word out,* and considering, person by person, the best ways to communicate with them. You tackled the important skill of learning to *make appointments* because one-on-one visits build your relationship, allow you to share your vision, provide prospects with opportunity to give, and help you develop prayer partners.

You prepared for your appointments by creating a script and learning how to *handle objections.* You prepared to *conduct the visit* by focusing on the memory device of six images: the photo album, road map, blueprint, globe, reading glasses, and uniform.

You learned to *track funds* and explored the important step of *saying* thank you. Expressing your gratitude needs to become a lifestyle.

You learned the alternate method of presenting your vision and ministry through *the phone appointment,* when meeting in person is not possible. You learned how to *expand your contacts* by asking your donors for referrals.

You discovered the absolute necessity of *cultivating your donors.* Continuing to build those important relationships becomes a fact of life for people raising funds. *Resoliciting funds* is a crucial part of ongoing fundraising, not to be overlooked.

With this quick review, you are ready to get serious about mastering six critical skills. This is where the rubber meets the road.

All of the steps you've covered in learning to raise funds by People Raising are important, but there are a handful of skills that have emerged as critical for your success. So let's go through each of these six crucial skills one at a time.

Critical Skill #1: Securing an Appointment over the Phone

I have continually emphasized the strategic importance of meeting in person. To get to that one-on-one meeting, though, you have to master the art of making the appointments. Review the materials in chapter 12 about developing and using your script. Remember that it's fine to adapt and modify your script, but without taking shortcuts.

Once you've got your script down, find someone you can practice with. Once you are ready to make some calls, practice on your low-priority contacts. Get the experience so that eventually you can focus on your high-priority, top ten contacts.

Critical Skill #2: Handling Phone Objections

Chapter 12 also laid out the common objections and various ways to handle them effectively. Get that practice partner, and brush up on responding to each of the objections. Keep in mind the two-step approach:

1. Recognize and respond to the objection, which is real in the prospect's mind.
2. Ask for the appointment again!

As you role-play, have your friend toss out the different objections, then make sure you come back with both step 1 and step 2.

Critical Skill #3: Conducting the Visit

Commit the six word pictures of Chapter 13 to memory; they can guide you through your presentation plan. In the middle of an appointment, when you're nervous, you might think, "What am I supposed to talk about next?" Then you recall the six word pictures. "That's right! The reading glasses are next." You can never practice enough on your presentation.

> *Commit the six word pictures to memory.*

The Photo Album. Bring the prospect up-to-date on your life, and catch up with what is going on in his or her life.

The Road Map. Tell your story, or testimony, of how God has led you into ministry.

The Globe. Tell how your organization fits God's kingdom purposes in world missions/world evangelization. Your goal is to show that you are connected with a well-respected organization in pursuit of God's agenda.

The Reading Glasses. Share your vision with excitement, focusing on what you want to accomplish for the Lord.

The Blueprint. Like a building requires blueprints, you have a plan for raising needed ministry funds. Talk about the steps you will take to meet your goal.

The Uniforms. The people in uniforms with your name on them represent your support team who give and pray for you. This is the point in your presentation when you ask the potential donor to join your team.

Critical Skill #4: Handling the Four Responses

Your coach or practice partner can help you practice handling each of the four responses you are likely to receive after you have specifically asked for support. Go back to chapter 13 and practice responding to each of these. Have your coach or practice partner state these responses so you can practice how you will respond in turn.

1. "Yes, I'd love to support you at $_____."
2. "Three hundred dollars is kind of high for me right now."
3. "I'd like to pray about it."
4. "No, I will not be able to support you."

Critical Skill #5: Asking for Referrals

Many fundraisers run out of contacts at some point in the process. Wouldn't it be great to be getting these referrals as you're working through the process? Donors who commit to support your vision for your ministry can be a great help in making new contacts. Review chapter 13 for how to ask for and collect solid referrals.

Critical Skill #6: Storytelling

The sixth skill is storytelling. As you paint a picture of a life being changed, listeners can readily relate to that. Isn't this the real reason donors give and continue to give? Everyone loves a good story of how God is at work in people's lives. This goes back to expressing your vision and not merely your need for funds. Paint a picture. Take every opportunity to tell a good story about your ministry. Incorporate these into a fundraising appointment, a church meeting, an informal get-together or dessert time, an interview with a missions committee, a newsletter, a prayer letter, an e-mail or phone update, and in your thank-you letters.

Take every opportunity to tell a good story about your ministry.

As you consider what kinds of stories to choose, look for stories that portray changed lives—either your own or the lives of people you serve—and stories that demonstrate how the funds you take into your ministry bring benefit to real people.

I am a firm advocate of storytelling. If you were to follow me around, you would hear me tell the stories of inner-city kids whose lives have been dramatically changed by the Lord. Many times there are tears in people's eyes as they hear firsthand the power of the gospel. But it is stories that paint that picture.

If you are brand-new to ministry you will need to get some stories from your organization. Even though they are not yours, people will understand. If you are currently in ministry, look for stories, write them down, and practice presenting them. Maintaining a diary is a good way of catching stories that need to be developed.

Now you've got the overview and your assignment. Everything hinges around these three things:

1. Your attitude toward fundraising
2. The skills you need to practice, and
3. Recognition that the Lord works above and beyond your strategies

CHAPTER 21

A Donor's Perspective on Fundraising

Throughout the People Raising strategy, I have emphasized the importance of relationships. A good fundraiser keeps the care of his prospects and donors as a central facet of his ministry. So what could be better than to get some insights into how a major donor thinks and reacts as he is challenged to give.

I took the opportunity to interview a major donor, and I am sure you will find the questions and his responses most helpful.

Can you give us some examples of good fundraisers you have encountered?
"Good fundraisers know who they are approaching, what their passions are, what relationships they have, and what they are interested in. They have done their homework. In addition, they care about persons more than their projects. While they know they have to "fish where the big fish are," they are more concerned with the owner of the pond than the fish they can catch.

"My all-time favorite story is the large donor who never gave his school a dime but was spiritually impacted by the fundraiser's compassion and care. To the best fundraisers, relationships are more important than mission. Good fundraisers know who to build a relationship with and how. They pay attention to the people around the prospective donor. They do not send a subordinate to do the job they should do, and they ignore the subordinates of the donor. They do not have an administrative assistant call to make an appointment. They call donors on birthdays and special occasions. They maintain relationships even if the donor no longer has the means to donate because the

"To the best fundraisers, relationships are more important than mission."

donor has become a friend. They have high emotional intelligence and know when 'No means no.'

"They view themselves as giving others an opportunity to invest rather than selling a commodity. Good fundraisers are comfortable around people of means. They are not jealous of the success of others and know how to socially adjust to a situation without compromising their values."

What are some of the things that really motivate you to give?

"Initiatives that are innovative and led by men and woman of character, compassion, and competence.

"Leaders who have a big vision, who lead by example, and who have personal righteousness, the ability to build relationships, and a visionary revelation that is world-impacting.

"Leaders who effectively answer the three questions of leadership:
1. Can I trust you?
2. Do you care about me?
3. Do you know what you want to do and can you do it?"

What makes a difference in whether you'll give or not give?

"I appreciate giving to initiatives where collaboration and creativity are involved and where lives are being changed rather than to programs or projects. I appreciate initiatives that are in line with our purpose, mission, and vision. I am interested in prevention more than rescue. I believe the 'truth will set us free,' and I am interested in initiatives that emphasize integrating truth into daily living."

What role do emotions play in your decision to give?

"While feelings play a role, ideally emotions should not be the driver; mission is. In fact, one of the reasons I will not commit 'on the spot' is to keep emotions from over-influencing the decision. To consistently make decisions on emotion would mean that we would be reactive contributors rather than strategic investors."

Do you prefer that people ask for a specific gift, a gift in a range, or not to be asked for a specific amount?

"Ask for a specific amount."

What does a good "ask" look like?

"[It includes five elements:]

1. It has a one- or two-page summary document clearly outlining the reasons for the project and its benefits.
2. It includes information as to who the beneficiaries are and what they have done to help the project.
3. There is information on what the "insiders" (board, staff, community, etc.) are sacrificially doing for the project.
4. There is a clear "ask" that is reasonable and specific.
5. There is a definite opportunity to say no without emotional consequences."

How important do you think follow-up is to a fundraiser?

"It's critical. While we are not the norm, we view ourselves as investors. Investors are "shareholders" in the organizations and people in which they invest. Reporting is essential."

The People Raising Connection

This top-ten donor touches on the topics emphasized in your People Raising strategy, which emphasizes relationships. He says, "Good fundraisers know who they are approaching, what their passions are, what relationships they have, and what they are interested in. They have done their homework." This donor reiterates the importance of fundraising as ministry to prospects and donors. He says, "They [fundraisers] care about persons more than their projects."

The donor also connects the fundraiser's follow-up as part of the relationship building, mentioning birthday cards or personal calls. He says, "Good fundraisers must be patient and build a relationship over time." Notice that the donor refers to himself as an "investor," in a relationship that naturally calls for reporting back about how his funds were used to accomplish your stated goals and mission.

I love this donor's perspective on the lasting nature of the friendship built between fundraiser and donor. He says, "They [fundraisers] maintain relationships even if the donor no longer has the means to donate because the donor has become a friend."

You'll notice, too, that the prospect doesn't find it a problem for you to ask for a specific amount. On the contrary, that's what this donor expects!

The donor's perspective can help you see the real value of all those personal notations you make in your fundraising diary, as you track the details of these lives and the significance that your thank-you carries in keeping that relationship growing. When you lose track of the big picture, remember why we call it People Raising. Come back to this chapter and shift your focus back to the relationships you're building with your donors. It will keep your efforts donor-focused.

CHAPTER 22

Coaching Can Make the Difference

Tom Landry, the well-known football coach of the Dallas Cowboys, once said, "A coach is someone that makes you *do* what you *don't want to do.*" The accountability aspect is a crucial part of the coach's role, though it is not the complete story. A good coach offers a fundraiser so much more, so let's explore the coach's critical role in the People Raising strategy.

It's possible that you, as a fundraiser, truly cannot secure a coach to come alongside you to help. I encourage you not to skip the principles presented in this chapter; they may help you coach yourself as you tackle key issues.

Why Coaching?

Most fundraisers are facing a task they have never attempted before: raising money. Fear and inexperience leave the fundraiser vulnerable and prone to make mistakes. Those mistakes lead to limited results and, usually, a serious case of discouragement. An uncoached fundraiser steps, potentially, onto a path of frustration. In the worst-case scenario when a fundraiser is not coached, he or she keeps on making the same mistakes, with results of no gift or minimal gifts, lost opportunities, and longer support-raising time.

The good news is that the frustration, discouragement, and dragged-out fundraising time are all preventable. In People Raising, there are two major roles the coach plays. Number one, the coach praises you, the fundraiser, for what you are doing right. Number two, the coach critiques you on what could be improved.

Webster's helps us by defining coaching as "training intensively, by

Frustration, discouragement, and a dragged-out fundraising time are all preventable.

instruction and demonstration." The coach is "a private tutor, one who instructs or trains."[1]

Now if the coach's job is to praise you on what's right and critique you about what needs improving, which I call troubleshooting, obviously it is very important that the coach has experience. For instance, I am able to coach others in their fundraising because I've actually raised funds and continue to raise funds and train others. Experience in raising funds is critical.

Baseball offers a good example. Let's say you know very little about baseball, but you've decided you'd like to be a pitcher. Someone recommends that you need a coach to hold you accountable. So you find a coach who will hold you accountable, but one who has little experience with baseball. He can ask key accountability questions, like "Did you read the baseball rule book?" or "How much time did you practice last week?" Such accountability is good, but what happens when other questions arise, such as "How do I throw a curveball, or a knuckleball?" and "Where is the strike zone?" The inexperienced coach offers little or no value in helping you answer these critical pitching questions.

Accountability is important, yet finding a coach merely to hold you accountable in your fundraising efforts is not going to cut it! I guarantee that as you go through this process you will run into many issues and questions, such as, "I have made a number of phone calls seeking appointments, but no one wants to meet with me. What should I do next?" or "I thought I had a good meeting with some prospects, but they said nothing about supporting me. Why do you think that was the case?" or "I am frustrated because I've run out of contacts. What in the world do I do next?" These and other questions need to be addressed by a person experienced in raising funds.

Profile of a Good Coach

Considering what makes a good coach will help you see that coaching isn't so simple or straightforward. The best coach is an *experienced fundraiser*, with *good one-on-one skills*. He or she is personally *disciplined* and is *encouraging, enthusiastic,* and *motivating*. The coach is *highly focused* and skilled at *holding the fundraiser accountable*. The coach is a *good listener,* a *creative* problem-solver, and a *prayer warrior*. Other roles of the good coach include strategist, counselor, pastor, encourager, teacher, mentor, fundraiser, manager, or detective.

Four Key Ingredients in the Funding Process

The coach helps you, the fundraiser, focus on four key ingredients. Whether you are raising $4,000 a month or $25,000 for your ministry, you need to be about these four key tasks.

1. Selecting names (constantly adding, prioritizing)
2. Getting appointments
3. Visiting/asking
4. Following up

These four ingredients form a permanent structure for fundraising, whether you're just beginning to raise funds or you've been at it for a long time.

Before the start of a junior-high basketball game, the coach gets the team on the court to practice free throws, layups, and other basic basketball skills. If you watch a high-school team on the court before their game, the players are doing the same thing. If you watch a college basketball team take the court prior to a game, they're going through the same drills. If you watch a pro basketball team take the floor before a game, they too would be practicing free throws, layups, and basic basketball skills.

No matter who you are or at what level you're engaged in your fundraising, you will constantly be *selecting names, getting appointments, visiting and making the ask*, and *following up.*

Troubleshooting the Four Key Ingredients

A fundraiser, together with his or her coach, will encounter issues connected with these four key ingredients that will need to be addressed. You as a fundraiser will depend on your coach for troubleshooting because it's difficult to diagnose your own problems; an objective mentor may be able to identify areas of breakdown and provide effective suggestions to solve the problems.

Selecting Names/Prospects

Troubles in this area stem from an incomplete list. People have been left off the list for one reason or another. There are just not enough names to prioritize and get started.

These issues are solved by going back to the teaching on compiling a strong contact list in chapter 9. Use that checklist on p. 73–74, and throw the net wide as you brainstorm. Don't stop brainstorming when you've thought of one or two people from church, and one or two from work. Cover every point on the checklist, and be as thorough as you can. Don't let negative thinking paralyze you. It is so easy to explain away why people should not be placed on your list. Remember to let your prospects make the decision whether they will support you, not you. Also go back and review how to expand your contacts (chapter 17), practicing getting referrals from current donors and maximizing the opportunity of an event such as the dessert time.

Getting Appointments

Recall the five components to getting appointments: (1) making the call, (2) asking for the appointment, (3) handling objections, (4) asking for the appointment again, and (5) confirming the appointment.

If you are having trouble getting appointments, a good coach can help you identify where the problem lies and then fix it!

1. *Making the Call.* Problems at this early step stem from either making too few calls or not getting through to the right person.

If the problem is that too few calls are being made, it could be that fear or laziness is a problem, or that you're lacking a sense of urgency. Attack this problem by praying about it. Imagine a worst-case scenario—that is, what is the worst that can happen when you pick up the phone and make that call. Then start with the easier calls, especially one that will almost certainly be a win. With the help of your coach, set some goals and deadlines for how many calls you will make.

Start with an easy call—a win!

The problem may be that you are not getting through to your prospects. This could simply be a matter of bad timing. Try various times of day and weekends. Increase the number of people being called to improve your percentage. Ask the people you do reach when is the best time to reach the prospect.

2. *Asking for the Appointment.* We learned in chapter 12 that this step can be tricky. The words you use and the tone and content of your conversation are important. Get a script written down, and then role-play with your coach. You can never do enough role-playing. Continue to go back to role-playing to get the scripting perfected.

3. *Handling Objections.* If you are having trouble making appointments because the prospects bring your conversation to a standstill, then you may be having problems with fear, with insufficient training, or with

> *You can never do enough role-playing.*

responding to new objections. It's important to tackle this issue before discouragement sets in. Ask God to calm your fear or nervousness, and remind yourself that you are about His business. Work with your coach, allowing him or her to look for ways to tweak your approach and improve your script. Go back to chapter 12 and have your coach work with you to handle the usual objections until your responses begin to be natural.

Discouragement is a point where a coach becomes a vital part of your fundraising process. When you're discouraged, your coach can come alongside with solutions to fix the troublesome issue and with help for training you to handle the objections that come your way.

4. *Asking for the Appointment Again.* Together with your coach, practice that two-step approach: Respond to the objection, and ask for the appointment again.

5. *Confirming the Appointment.* A coach may discover that you as the fundraiser didn't finish the appointment call well or follow through afterward. The phone call should end with your confirmation of the date and time that you have agreed on to meet with the prospect or with setting up a time when you will get back in touch with this particular prospect to ask for an appointment again. The next step is to send an e-mail or a letter if necessary to firm up what you've settled over the phone.

A coach may find that you are taking no too easily, or that you are failing to make confirmation of your appointment. Get back to role-playing, so the coach can see where your follow-up isn't working and so you can practice getting the final stage of making the appointment right.

Visiting and Asking

There are three disturbing trends that you or the coach needs to be looking out for.

The first is *few gifts coming in.* The questions for the coach to explore are "Is the fundraiser asking?" and "Is the fundraiser contacting the right people?". The coach needs to analyze the ask.

The second trend is *few pledge gifts and more special gifts.* The coach can make sure the fundraiser is asking for a pledged gift. Analyze the ask.

The third trend is *size of the gifts is on the low end.* A coach might ask you: Are you asking for a specific amount or in a range? Are you using a $100 minimum ask? Are you raising people's vision by asking for a higher gift? Are you making a second ask in a lower range?

The ask is the central issue. You need to review, tweak, role-play, and do all that it takes to make this work for you.

Following Up

Follow-up is critical, and I'm convinced a lot of gifts are lost because this step is not properly executed. Keep in mind that the fundraiser's goal is to bring the prospect or donor to a decision. When a person asks for more time to consider a gift, don't forget the 48-Hour Rule. But set it up, follow it up, and keep on following it up.

A good coach can hold you accountable in this area of pursuing a giving decision, and can help you identify the problem if you are failing to bring your prospect or donor to a decision.

Three Phases of the Coaching Process

You have probably begun to see how essential an experienced coach can be as you raise funds. Your coach-fundraiser teamwork will develop through three phases.

Phase 1: The Initial Training

At a first meeting, both coach and fundraiser will:

1. Review the People Raising strategy, focusing on reducing the fear and reducing the time. Purchase the People Raising training seminar with Study guide, available in CD, DVD, and MP3 (www.peopleraising.com).
2. Exchange contact information such as e-mail addresses, cell phone, and Skype numbers.
3. Commit to each other.
4. Set a time for weekly meeting and reports.
5. Bring current fears and questions to the surface.
6. Sign up the fundraiser for a free monthly People Raising newsletter (www.peopleraising.com).

The coach will give a homework assignment. A recommended first assignment would be for the coach to establish a deadline for the fundraiser to view the six-hour DVD of the People Raising training program and to complete the study guide.

As follow-up to the first meeting, the coach will compile information about the fundraiser, keeping track of the contact details (e-mail, cell phone numbers, etc.) and beginning a diary that will help track the progress the fundraiser is making and the issues that need to be dealt with.

A simple agenda for the second meeting between the coach and the fundraiser would include:

1. Answer any questions.
2. Review the fundraiser's responses to the study guide.
3. Provide further training.
4. Assign homework.
5. Schedule the next meeting.

The coach's follow-up is to add to the diary and then send the fundraiser a memo providing encouragement and restating the goals and deadlines for the next meeting.

Phase 2: Preparing the Fundraiser to Launch

In regular meetings with the fundraiser, the coach will help the fundraiser

1. Review the prospect list.
2. Role-play making the appointment.
3. Role-play handling objections.
4. Role-play making the "ask."
5. Role-play acknowledging the four responses.
6. Review asking for referrals.
7. Discuss the week just past, and create a plan for the week ahead.

Obviously, a lot of the time you'll be practicing. Don't move forward until you, as fundraiser, are handling the phone script, objections, the "ask," and the responses with confidence. A premature start will end up with frustration and mistakes. Take the needed time to prepare; it will provide huge dividends.

You'll find the reports we're going to talk about later in this chapter helpful in discussing progress made

Take the needed time to prepare; it will provide huge dividends.

during the previous week and establishing a plan for the week ahead.

Phase 3: Monitoring the Plan

The coach will have the fundraiser submit weekly reports by an agreed date and time. These need to be submitted by e-mail in advance of the appointment, allowing the coach an opportunity to review the report prior to the meeting, which can take place *in person, by phone,* or *by Skype.* Ahead of time, the coach will also review his diary of notes regarding the fundraiser's progress and ideas for fine-tuning the strategy.

The coach then conducts the weekly coaching sessions, during which

1. The fundraiser provides his evaluation of the past week.
2. The coach offers his insights as he reviews the fundraiser's report on the past week.
3. The coach provides input from his or her diary.
4. Coach and fundraiser finalize strategy for the next week.
5. The coach assigns homework.

After each meeting, the coach will update information and comments into his diary and will send the fundraiser a memo, including praise and constructive criticism as well as homework and deadlines.

Weekly Reporting

The following six weekly reports provide both the fundraiser and the coach a good picture of where they have been, where they are currently, and a plan for the week ahead.

Prospect and Donor Information

The first report is a donor roster. (See sample on next page.) Here is where you keep track of key information on your prospects and donors. You would want to capture the basics, such as:

Last name, first name

Profession/position

Number of family incomes

Priority (high, medium, low)

Top 10 (Does the prospect
    qualify for this group?)

Address (with city, state, zip)

Business address

Salutation

Phone numbers (home, work,
    and cell)

E-mail address

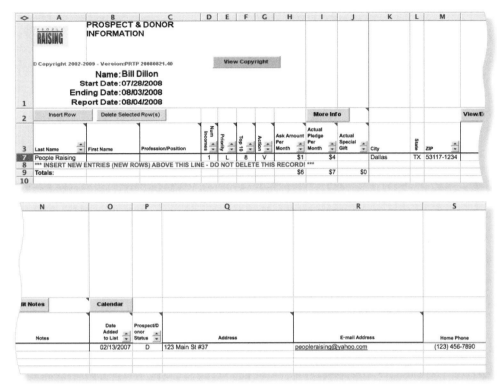

Spouse's name

Name of personal assistant

Referred by

Date added to the list

Church attended

Lifestyle (vacations, cars, etc.)

Note about your relationship
   with donor

Action to be taken

Visit

Ask for the appointment

Letter/phone strategy

New names

"Ask" amount

"Ask" amount per month

Actual pledge per month

Actual special gift

WEEKLY PLANNING REPORT-[NEXT WEEK]

© Copyright 2002-2008 · Version:PRTP 20080821.40

Name: Bill Dillon
Starting Date: 08/04/2008
Ending Date: 08/10/2008
Report Date: 08/04/2008

Name	Phone For Appointment	Conduct 1-On-1 Visit	Send Letter	Phone Appeal	Phone Follow-Up	Group Presentation	Donor Advocate	Follow Up Undecided	Amount to Request	Notes
Kendall, Forrest	X		X			X			$25	
Doe, John		X		X			X	X	$75	
People Raising			X			X			$150	line 1 line 2 line 3 line 4 line 5 line 6 line 7
*** INSERT NEW ENTRIES (NEW ROWS) ABOVE THIS LINE - DO NOT DELETE THIS RECORD! ***										
Weekly Total Amount Requested									$250	

Insert Row / Delete Selected Row(s) / View/Edit Notes — Action to Be Taken — Letter/Phone Strategy

Weekly Planning Report

The second report is the weekly planning report (sample shown above.) In this report, you list your plan for the next week. You list the prospects you want to contact and the action you will take. Here are the possible actions:

Phone for an appointment.
Conduct the one-on-one visit.
Send a letter.
Make a phone appeal.
Follow up by phone.
Make a group presentation.
Contact a donor for a referral.
Follow up with the undecided.

After each name, you will want to put the amount you plan to request and any notes that will be helpful.

Report on the Past Week

The third report is the weekly report for the past week (see page 201). This report just reiterates the plan from last week and what have been the results. Last week you anticipated the amount you would request from an individual; this report will record the amount requested, the amount of the pledged gift or the amount of the special gift, and a note recording when you sent out a thank-you letter. You will include what follow-up is required, in case that prospect was unreached or undecided. You have a section for notes.

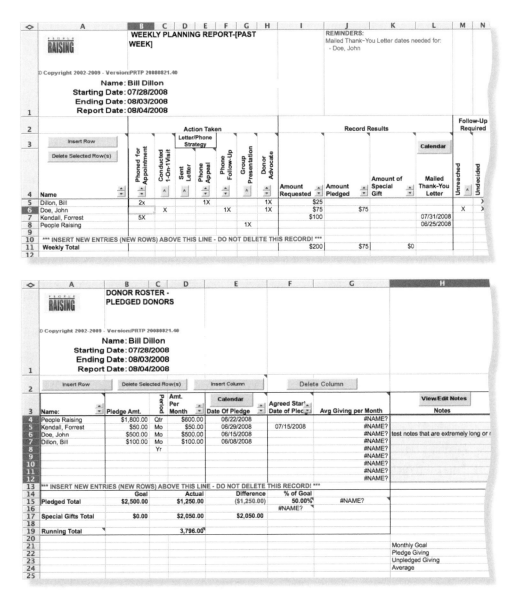

Donor Roster: Pledged Donors

This fourth report lists all your pledged donors, the pledged amount, the frequency of the pledge (monthly, quarterly, or annually), the amount per month for calculating purposes, the date the donor made the pledge, the agreed start date of the pledge, and the actual giving by month, as well as a note section. This allows you to keep track of people who, for one reason or another, don't send their pledged donation in.

	A	B	C	D	E	G	H	I	J	K
	RAISING	**DONOR ROSTER - SPECIAL GIFT DONORS**								
	© Copyright 2002-2009 - Version:PRTP 20080821.40									
		Name: Bill Dillon								
		Starting Date: 07/28/2008								
		Ending Date: 08/03/2008								
1		Report Date: 08/04/2008								
	Insert Row		Insert Column			Actual Giving by Month				
2	Delete Selected Row(s)		Delete Column							
			Total of	Calendar	View/Edit Notes					
3	Name	Giving Interest	Special Gifts	Date of Initial Gift	Notes	May-08	Jun-08	Jul-08	Aug-08	Sep-08
4	Kendall, Forrest		$700.00	06/01/2008	Showed some interest in a new compu		$300			
5	Dillon, Bill		$550.00				$550			
6	Doe, John		$700.00				$700			
7	People Raising		$100.00				$100			
8			$0.00							
9			$0.00							
10	*** INSERT NEW ENTRIES (NEW ROWS) ABOVE THIS LINE - DO NOT DELETE THIS RECORD! ***									
11		Goal	Actual	Difference						
12										
13	Special Gifts Total	$0.00	$2,050.00	$2,050.00		$0	$1,650	$0	$0	$(
14										
15	Pledged Total	$2,500.00	$1,250.00	($1,250.00)		$495	$851	$0	$0	$(
16										
17	Running Total		$3,396.00			$495	$2,501	$0	$0	$0
18										

Donor Roster: Special-Gift Donors

This fifth report identifies those who have given a special gift, including nota-tions of any kind of giving interests the donors have. For example, the donor may have given to cover a new computer or a car. Include the date of their initial gift. There is a note section here as well. Record by month the actual special giving.

Weekly Time Log

This sixth report breaks down each day by hour and date, to track how you are using your time during the fundraising process. The essential focus goes back to the key four ingredients: (1) selecting names (constantly adding, prioritiz-ing); (2) getting appointments; (3) visiting/asking; and (4) following up.

Put in this log a fifth category: "Other Fundraising Activities." This would include, for example, time spent on appeal letter, newsletter, and time spent in prayer for donors/fundraising activity. Keeping track of the time spent in each of these areas will provide the coach with a clear indication of how fo-cused you are as a fundraiser.

	A	B	C	D	E	F	G	H	
◇	A	B	C	D	E	F	G	H	

WEEKLY TIME LOG

RAISING

© Copyright 2002-2009 - Version:PRTP 20080821.40

	Name:	Bill Dillon							
	Starting Date:	07/28/2008							
	Ending Date:	08/03/2008							
1	Report Date:	08/04/2008							
2	Day		Action Taken	Calling for Appointments	Appointment With Donors	Phone Follow-Up	Working on New Names	Other Fundraising Activities	
124	9:00								
126	11:00								
127	Saturday		Daily Summary of Time Allotment	0	0	0	0		
128									
129	Sunday	Date:	8/3/08						
130	6:00								
131	7:00								
132	8:00								
133	9:00								
134	10:00								
135	11:00								
136	12:00								
137	1:00								
138	2:00								
139	3:00								
140	4:00								
141	5:00								
142	6:00								
143	7:00								
144	8:00								
145	9:00								
146	10:00								
147	11:00								
148	Sunday		Daily Summary of Time Allotment	0	0	0	0		
149									
150	Total Hours		WEEKLY Summary of Time Allotment	0	0	0	0		
151			WEEKLY % of Time Allotment	0.0%	0.0%	0.0%	0.0%		
152									

The Coach's Challenge:
Create Good Habits and Avoid Bad Habits

A habit is defined as "an acquired mode of behavior that has become nearly or completely involuntary."[2] There are two key words in that definition, the word *acquired* and the word *involuntary*. As People Raising techniques become habitual, fundraising becomes second nature. Here are ten good habits you can establish as you go about People Raising:

1. *Prioritize your contacts,* both old and new. This reduces the time it takes in the fundraising process. Catalogue individuals by high, medium, and low priority.

2. *Focus on your Top 10.* This reduces the time it takes to raise funds. Constantly review your Top 10. This list can be very fluid—names can go off, names can go on. But the Top 10 helps you to focus on those who can make the biggest difference through their giving.

3. *Keep adding names.* This also reduces the time it takes to raise funds.

4. *Keep thanking people.* This reduces donor turnover. Keep in mind that for every 100 people who stop supporting you, 66 percent think you don't care about them. That is something you can control. Other results: Happy donors who are appreciated are prime candidates to be asked to upgrade their giving. These added funds reduce the time it takes to raise funds.

5. *Start getting people to give immediately.* This helps you build up your account, which can provide funds for emergencies and special projects.

6. *Keep asking, "What is the next step* for this particular prospect or donor?" This maximizes your opportunities.

7. *Always start with the ideal.* For example, in following up names provided by a donor as a referral, the ideal scenario is for you, your donor, and the new referral prospect to meet. If the ideal is impossible, then work your way down from the ideal.

8. *Keep gathering data on your prospects and donors.* What churches do they attend? What do they do for a living?

9. *Keep recording information for future reference.*

10. *Keep raising people's vision.*

At the same time, there are bad habits you should avoid. Be aware of and stir clear of these four:

1. When making the appointments, ***don't tell your whole story.*** If you do, the prospect might not feel there is any need to meet.

2. *Avoid the group ask.* In the group setting, people tend to lowball their giving. When approached individually and challenged personally, they will give much more.

3. *Avoid asking too low.* When low, people asked will readily respond and do exactly what you asked them to do. But when you ask high, you have the chance to pull up the prospect's or donor's vision and giving.

4. *Don't raise funds without complete training.* For example, those who have not been trained in how to secure an appointment will be unable to get the appointments, will get discouraged, and will give up readily. Obviously, if you can't get the appointment, you can't personally ask people for their gifts.

Motivating the Fundraiser

Seven Keys to Motivating the Fundraiser

No matter who we are or what we do, there is always the concern of being motivated or how to motivate others. Here are seven keys to motivating the fundraiser. Keep in mind, you're always trying to reduce the time and fear involved in fundraising.

1. *Training.* Give the fundraiser a plan.

2. *Get off to a good start.* Create some wins.

3. *Establish deadlines*—urgency with accountability.

4. *Remove barriers*—anything/anyone that comes between you and the decision maker.

5. *Create giving models.* Based on what the fundraiser has accomplished so far and what the future goal is, you can project how long it might take to see the goal accomplished. This has several benefits. In some cases, it's a wake-up call in that the fundraiser has to put in more time and focus. It can also serve as an encouragement, because the fundraiser can see that the fundraising task is doable.

6. *Provide tech support.* As a coach, make yourself available to the fundraiser. When troubles come, the fundraiser can get in touch quickly so you can help solve problems and keep the fundraiser motivated. Failing to provide this accessibility indicates that the next time you meet, you'll have to address more issues, provide more correction. Meanwhile, the fundraiser may become discouraged and nonproductive until your next coaching session.

7. *Create policies that encourage motivation.* It is my belief that those in ministry should not be allowed to engage in their ministry assignments until 100 percent of their support is raised. Both the coach and the fundraiser want them to get to their assignment as quickly as possible. But if you allow them to get to their assignments prematurely, without 100 percent of their support, you've just removed their major motivation to complete their fundraising.

Effective Questioning

As a coach, you will make better progress with your fundraiser if you shape your questions specifically rather than in general terms. For instance,

Wrong: "How did your fundraising calls go?"

Right: "What decisions did each of your three prospects make?"

You will find that it's an important part of your job to press for detail as your fundraiser reports. You might ask:

"What do you mean?"

"Can you be more specific?"

"Give me an example."

"On a scale of 1 to 10, how is your fear factor?"

A Covenant between Coach and Fundraiser

Yes, coaching can make a difference. But you need a plan and a strategy that is embraced by the coach and the fundraiser and followed through on a consistent basis. Every effective partnership requires commitment. At the earliest phase of your relationship with your coach, I suggested that the two of you commit to each other. Campus Crusade offers the following useful statements—one for the fundraiser, one for the coach—that make a great place to start.[3]

New Staff Member

As a new staff member raising my initial support, I commit myself to the following:

1. I will be available for our phone appointments. If an extenuating circumstance arises, I will call or e-mail you before our appointment to ask to reschedule it.
2. I will complete my MPD [ministry partner development] Weekly Update every week and submit it by Sunday midnight.
3. I will follow through with what you ask me to do.
4. I will let you know if you say something that hurts me or angers me. I will also let you know if I disagree with you. I commit to keeping a "short account" with you.
5. I will get your approval for any travel, conferences, and retreats, and any other non-MPD ministry activity (i.e., weekly meetings, staff planning meeting).
6. I will talk with you before taking another job.
7. I will trust God to meet all of my needs. If I had debt before coming on staff, I will not increase it.
8. I will consult with you first before making any major purchases.
9. I will believe the best in you.
10. I will work hard and consider MPD a full-time job (forty-plus hours each week).
11. I will create a prayer letter each month and e-mail you a copy.
12. I will take some time off each week.

_____   _____

New Staff Member's Signature   Date

Ministry Partner Development Coach

As your MPD Coach I commit myself to the following:

1. I will believe the best in you.
2. I will keep you accountable.
3. I will pray regularly for you.
4. I will be available for our phone appointments. If an extenuating circumstance arises, I will call or e-mail you before our appointment to ask to reschedule it.
5. I will speak the truth in love even if it is hard.
6. I will let you know if you say something that hurts or angers me. I commit to keeping a "short account" with you.
7. I am available for your questions.
8. I will rejoice in God's provision and celebrate with you.

_____   _____
Coach's Signature   Date

Reading this chapter as a fundraiser or coach, you see the importance of proper and complete preparation, troubleshooting, and ongoing commitment and focus. Be committed and move forward.

CHAPTER 23

The Role of Prayer in Fundraising

Jesus said it Himself: "Apart from me you can do nothing" (John 15:5). This applies to fundraising as well. Dr. Howard Hendricks has said, "Prayer is recognition that my need is not partial; it is total."

For the fundraiser, focus on prayer takes on two dimensions. The first dimension is the prayer life of the fundraiser. The second is the prayer support needed by the fundraiser to sustain his ministry.

The Fundraiser's Prayer Life

Every step in our fundraising planning and execution has to be bathed in prayer. If this is the Lord's ministry, then it's important that we consult with Him—regarding our need for funds and to praise Him for the successes we experience.

Let's think through some of the many ways prayer needs to intersect with your fundraising.

As You Build Your Prospect List

Pray that the Lord will go before you, quickening and preparing the hearts of your prospects, as you set out to make the connection with those who may become part of your team.

Steve Shadrach wrote about building a prospect list:

> I just finished making a list of people I want to approach this month. I'm asking some to join our monthly team for the first time, others to restart, and a few regular givers to consider increasing. My plan is

all in place, except for one minor detail. I haven't 'made my requests known to God' as commanded in Philippians 4:6. A Christian leader once said to me, "We must talk to God about men before we talk to men about God." The Lord will go before us and open doors and hearts—but He wants us to *ask* Him to do it![1]

In the early days of my Inner City Impact ministry I mentally listed key people with whom I hoped to meet someday. They were people whom God had blessed who could help financially if they caught our vision. I prayed that someday they would help bring hope to inner-city children and their families. In particular, I prayed for one man.

Several years later a friend urged me to attend a banquet of another non-profit organization. He mentioned that his friend was hosting a table and was looking for another couple to attend.

Interested, I asked who the table host was. To my amazement, it was the

Pray for key people to join your team.

man I had been praying to meet. I accepted the invitation and exchanged business cards with the table host. Several years later he toured our ministry facilities and eventually became a significant donor. God can perform miracles as you raise your funds. Begin to pray today for key people to join your team.

As You Call to Set Up Appointments

You will find it natural to pray as you set out to make calls. Your nervousness or fear will drive you to seek help from above. That moment before you pick up the phone is the perfect time to ask God to help you be calm, to focus on your ministry to the prospect on the other end of the line, to go before you. Your faith will grow as you see God with you at each step of the fundraising process.

As You Conduct the Visit

I love the story of Nehemiah. He stands out in my mind because he was an urban planner. His management of rebuilding the walls of Jerusalem serves as a management model for us to replicate.

Back in March or April, 444 B.C., Nehemiah served as the king's cupbearer, holding a trusted position in the king's administration. In performing his duties, Nehemiah appeared daily before the king. One day, noting that

Nehemiah appeared sad, the king asked him, "Why does your face look so sad when you are not ill? This can be nothing but sadness of heart" (Nehemiah 2:2).

What was on Nehemiah's mind was the destruction of Jerusalem. When Nehemiah explained this to the king, the king basically said, "Well, how can I help you?" (Nehemiah 2:4, paraphrased). Nehemiah's automatic response was awesome. Scripture tells us two things happened. First, Nehemiah prayed to the God of heaven, and then he replied to the king.

It must have taken great courage for Nehemiah to share his vision for the rebuilding of Jerusalem. Like Nehemiah, there will be countless occasions when you *Stop and pray, right then and there.* will be plain scared when confronted with an issue or a question. Do like Nehemiah. Stop and pray, right then and there, as you hear the question of the potential donor.

As You Speak and Share in Public Meetings

Ask God to help you be discerning about when and where to present your ministry in public. Dr. Ernest Gambrell wrote,

> Missionaries have driven many miles and gone to some churches where God did not want them. They wasted time and money. . . . The ministry of deputation is not a happenstance ministry. Just as surely as God calls a certain missionary to a certain country, He also has certain churches He selects to support that ministry. It is important that the missionary seeks God's guidance for open doors and invitations to share his burden.[2]

You will pray before, during, and after these public presentations of your ministry. Acknowledge that God is the one who will prompt listeners to become supporters of your work, and trust Him for the outcome.

As You Experience Disappointment

In a perfect world, 100 percent of the people you call would not only give you an appointment but would also make a financial commitment. That is not going to happen. At times of discouragement, turn back in prayer, asking for God's continued direction.

As You Celebrate

Every time you conduct a successful donor appointment, every time you receive a positive response, every time you accept a generous gift, take the time to stop and pray and give God the glory.

As You Minister to Your Donors

Your donors' lives are like yours, filled with ups and downs. They have their own problems and heartaches. Your prayer on their behalf is essential. You and your ministry need prayer support, but remember that relationships operate on a two-way street. Your supporters are praying for you, and you need to pray sincerely for them. One ministry leader wrote, "As you solicit the prayer support of others, you must accept the responsibility of praying for them."[3]

Viewing people merely as prospects is cold and artificial. You are relating to needy people who need someone to minister to them. You may be God's chosen person to meet those needs. Listen as they talk, and record their requests on your prayer list. Love them. Pray for them.

I had a delightful lunch recently with one of our donors. As we talked, he thanked me several times for some advice I had given him months before. "It was," he said, "exactly what I needed as I serve on our church board." It encouraged me to see the support relationship working both ways.

God has given each of us a tremendous ministry with donors. Pray for those who support you—for their careers, marriages, families, and churches.

The mission board of Pioneers offers the following suggestions for praying for donors.[4]

1. Develop your own strategy and system for praying for each supporter.
2. Keep a picture album as you pray for families with children.
3. Make praying for donors a regular part of your devotions. To help you be systematic, put names of donors on different dates of the calendar, and pray for them on those dates.
4. In your prayer letters ask supporters to send you specific prayer requests.

As You Travel

Your fundraising will involve some travel, whether the distances are short or long.

For some, travel means going thousands of miles by car and by air. So pray for safe passage and weather conditions, and that the car will work. We drive defensively and pray that the Lord will protect us from reckless drivers.

A former pastor tells the story of a friend who woke up in the middle of the night and felt compelled to pray specifically for his pastor. When the pastor returned, he learned of the man's middle-of-the-night prayer at exactly the time when he was in a situation of danger.

When a missionary has a support team of prayer warriors, the Holy Spirit will burden them to action at exactly the times when the prayers are needed, although the one praying may be unaware of the needs. That is a miracle—and the results that follow will be miracles as well.

When You Drop the Ball

There are going to be times when you find yourself regretting your own failures. Maybe you will fail to put in the effort in raising funds, or maybe you will neglect to thank your supporters. These times also call for prayer. Talk to your heavenly Father and confess your shortcomings.

Praying Without Ceasing

Prayer ought to become part of the fundraiser's DNA.

Dr. Ernest Gambrell puts prayer at the center of fundraising: "The ministry of deputation should be based upon and begin, as all other ministries, with prayer!"[5] Needless to say, for the fundraiser, our motto ought to be "Pray without ceasing" (1 Thessalonians 5:17 NKJV). Prayer needs to be part of the fundraiser's DNA. It should be a lifestyle.

The Prayer Support Needed by the Fundraiser

The fundraiser needs the consistent prayer support of family, friends, and the body of Christ. We are in a spiritual battle, and spiritual battles need spiritual weapons. Prayer is one of those weapons.

In many corners of the world today, ordinary people undertake extraordinary tasks for Jesus Christ. Part of the secret of their fruitful ministry is that they are bathed in faithful prayer by God's people, whether those prayer warriors are nearby or far away. Many people do not realize the extent of the battle Satan wages. "Our struggle is not against flesh and blood," wrote the apostle Paul, "but against the rulers, against the authorities, against the powers of this world and against the spiritual forces of evil in the heavenly realms" (Ephesians 6:12).

Because of the many demands on your time and the special need for prayer in your ministry, you need many others to uphold you in prayer in a vital intercessory ministry, even as you take on this same role of prayer supporter for other friends involved in kingdom ministry. When your prayer supporters take seriously the responsibility of carrying this prayer burden, your victories and triumphs are theirs to share.

The following suggestions, adapted from Greater Europe Mission's materials, may help your donors as they bring you before the Lord in prayer. Your supporters might pray for you and your ministry using these same categories: thanks, daily life, barriers, time, Holy Spirit, family, and help.

Thanks

Thank God for His call and for the fundraiser's obedience to God's leading. Thank Him for the privilege of being involved in His work by upholding them in prayer. Express thanks for the known blessings in their lives, for successes in the ministry in terms of conversions and spiritual growth. Thank God for His faithfulness in hearing your prayers on their behalf.

Daily Life

The ministry worker's common problems are the same as yours; they are subject to the same temptations and weaknesses you are. When you face problems, pray for your missionary or ministry worker in those same areas of life. Pray about loneliness. Pray that the worker will be kept from pride, personality conflicts, and discouragement. Pray that he or she will be able to serve effectively with fellow workers.

Barriers

Pray that God will minimize or remove any obstacles in the ministry worker's work and relationships. Some of these may be cross-cultural. Pray that the efforts of Satan will meet with failure. Pray that your ministry worker will not experience hostility or persecution. Pray that the Lord will keep His servants faithful in His Word and safe from the attacks of the enemy.

Time

Pray that your ministry worker will use his or her time wisely. Most are busy people with many demands on their lives. The task is always greater than their ability to serve, and it is very difficult to say no. Ask God to help your ministry worker discern which activities are most important in God's economy. Pray especially that your ministry workers will get much-needed rest for their bodies and minds, that they might be alert and effective in their work.

Holy Spirit

Ask that the Holy Spirit will lead your servant leader to prepared hearts. Although some hearts resist the gospel, many are hungry for spiritual reality. Ask God to bring your ministry worker into contact with those people. Pray that these hearts will be released from the grasp of doubt and fear and rebellion against God.

Family

Parents can be torn between ministry and family demands, especially when the family is serving in a foreign culture, where cross-cultural differences can magnify everyday crises. Pray for family peace and harmony.

Help

Most workers serve in a way that can only touch the tip of the iceberg in terms of the real needs that exist. Pray for more workers to join the ministry. Jesus told His disciples to pray that "the Lord of the Harvest would send forth laborers into the fields." There are never enough workers to complete the job. Pray that God will call new resources into His service and that more workers will dedicate themselves in obedience to Him.[6]

Greater Europe Mission urges prayer supporters to "select a regular time to pray, and pray with diligence . . . [making it] a time of carrying their burdens to the Lord."[7] Obviously, this level of praying means the prayer supporter will have to stay in close contact, which is much easier with e-mail, Skype, and the introduction of social media applications. The prayer supporter can keep up with the ministry worker's current needs, no matter how far apart the worker and the prayer supporter are geographically. The praying supporter can be in touch, writing to ask about ministry specifics or what developments have taken place regarding an issue they've been praying about.

Sometimes it's hard for prayer supporters to know *how* to pray beyond the generic "God bless Rob and Jill." The following helpful guide from Missionary Tech provides prayer topics the prayer supporter can fit into a daily devotional time.[8] Prayer supporters might take their pick or use all three.

Sunday: Relationship with God

- Awareness of God's power
- Good times in His Word
- Conformity to His desire

Monday: Physical needs
- General health
- Financial supply
- Strength and safety for work

Tuesday: Relationships with others
- Ability to submit to one another
- Honesty, openness
- Appreciation of others' gifts

Wednesday: Effective ministry
- Open doors for ministry
- Good use of time
- Personal witness

Thursday: Family life
- A healthy marriage
- Happy, secure children
- Good communication with parents, brothers, sisters

Friday: Emotional needs
- Healthy self-esteem
- Satisfaction in ministry
- Growth as a person

Saturday: Spiritual walk
- Assurance of Father's love
- Sense of Christ's presence
- Submission to Holy Spirit

The Prayer/Advisory Group

Another prayer tool is the prayer/advisory group, a team of supporters who fulfill the scriptural principles regarding praying before making plans and having others pray with you. Wycliffe Bible Translators reports that some have found the creation of such a team of supporters "the most significant thing they have done in support raising."[9]

No matter where you are serving for God's kingdom, you need this team of prayer partners, who become so invested in helping you plan and prioritize and pray for your ministry, that they "develop a sense of ownership in ministry results. They also may act as advocates, make referrals, and fill special roles for which they are uniquely gifted or experienced."[10]

Wycliffe indicates that the central focus of this group is to develop "a spiritual approach to mutual ministry." They describe the purpose of your home prayer team: "to get others to meet with you in worship, praise, and adoration before the Lord and then to pray, specifically, about problems, possible solutions, and priorities."[11]

Remember the teaching of Ecclesiastes that "Two are better than one, because they have a good return for their work" (4:9). Your prayer/advisory group becomes a team that offers a practical, spiritual foundation for your efforts. "Your confidence in being in the Lord's will, with His timing, and sharing the load with others, will significantly increase your effectiveness in meeting the needs of others, both among those who send you and among those to whom you are sent."[12]

Creating the Prayer Team

Here are some tips to create this group of key prayer partners.

1. *Consider geography.* The personal and interactive quality of this support team makes close proximity important. The team needs to be together, in person, in prayer. If you have committed prayer warrior supporters in more than one area, you might want to have two groups.

2. *Be flexible about time commitment.* Some prayer support groups work together to get a ministry worker launched and then disband. That's fine, as long as you have another prayer support group that wants to pray for you long-term. Naturally, life circumstances may make members of this group drop out, and other supporters may want to join in. It's expected that the group members may fluctuate a bit, but it would be best to continue to have a group focused on prayer support.

3. *Focus on strong leadership.* You have other work to do. You will not be the leader of this group. So it'll be important to find a person who is passionate about your ministry to take charge of the group. This person will even be the one who collects others and asks them to become part of your prayer/advisory group. "Pray about a leader for the group. . . . he will be the key in making the group work effectively. The leadership of the Antioch church fasted and prayed after the Spirit had identified Barnabas and Saul as their missionaries (Acts 13:1-3). Note there was a sense of responsibility to God, above the needs of the missionaries."[12]

4. *Keep the group small and select.* The members of this prayer team are committing to your work at a high level. Four or five people to pray and advise may be just about right.[13] Members of this prayer support team may or may not all come from one sending church. Sometimes a team that has been pulled from more than one context provides wisdom in balance.

5. *Get out of the way.* You as ministry worker should be quick to bring issues and problems to this group for prayer, but experience with such groups shows that it's better for you *not* to bring your possible solutions to the group for their stamp of approval. If your prayer team has the chance to pray over the issues and problems, there is a possibility that through prayer, God will lead the group to recommend solutions that may or may not look like the ones you've already got in mind. Let your prayer team share the spiritual work of seeking God's leading.

6. *Remember who is really in charge.* Your prayer team's leader will be key in helping the group keep its focus on God as the author and finisher of our faith and of all His plans for your ministry. You are not the ultimate authority. Your team's leader is not, either. As a group, this prayer team is seeking the Lord's authority and wisdom, every time they meet.

7. *Keep it advisory, not directive.* If your prayer team comes up with solutions that will not mesh with your ministry policies or your organization's parameters, you will continue to follow the guidelines of your ministry. Your prayer team's role is to pray and advise, but not necessarily to steer the ship.[14]

8. *Be patient.* Group dynamics take time, and it may take awhile until this prayer/advisory team is functioning smoothly and effectively. Help your chosen team leader in every way you can, and then wait to see how it shapes up.

Two-Way Partnership

As they catch and begin to share your vision for ministry, your prayer team members may find great personal satisfaction in taking a greater role in fulfilling the Great Commission through your work. The ministry truly becomes mutual, with accountability working both ways. Wycliffe lays out the responsibilities that work both ways.

You, as ministry worker, are accountable for

1. Keeping the group fully aware of all situations concerning the partnership

2. Carrying out plans as agreed

3. Reporting progress, results, answers to prayer, and so on[15]

Your prayer team's central tasks are worship and prayer, focusing on seeking God's wisdom for your ministry. Your prayer team may also take on other advisory roles, being accountable for

1. Relating to others to obtain help in several areas of problem-solving

2. Helping you set appointments with key people, such as pastors, church leaders, mission committees, and so on

3. Taking active steps in the development of financial solutions, not necessarily from personal resources but by involving others

4. Assisting with scheduling, hosting, and follow-up of home meetings, or scheduling interviews with key people[16]

A Practical Plan of Action

Wycliffe Bible Translators offers the following outline to help ministry workers get a prayer/advisory team started.[17]

    I. Pray! Get others to pray with you.

    II. Choose names for prospective leader and group members from:

        A. Financial partners

        B. Prayer partners

        C. Potential financial partners

        D. Church leaders (pastor, elder, missions committee chairperson).

    III. Make the contact by mail, phone, or e-mail

        A. You or someone else writes.

        B. You or someone else follows up with a phone call.

    IV. Obtain commitment.

    V. Equip and prepare the group leader.

    VI. Set goals and a schedule for meeting goals (set target date).

    VII. Follow up regularly (personal visits, phone calls, letters).

    VIII. Maintenance

        A. Newsletters (plan occasional reference to and recognize the group)

        B. Prayer letters (give feedback, answers to prayer, etc.)

        C. Consider using copies of your monthly financial statement to keep the leader current. This allows him to carry responsibility of new effort in case of loss of partner, quota increase, etc.

D. Send personal thank-you notes regularly.

E. Be sure the group is consulted before any decisions are made impacting the partnership.

Take It to the Lord in Prayer

As you raise funds, claim Psalm 121. I call it "the fundraiser's prayer":

I lift up my eyes to the hills—where does my help come from?
My help comes from the Lord, the Maker of heaven and earth.
He will not let your foot slip—he who watches over you will not slumber;
    indeed, he who watches over Israel will neither slumber nor sleep.
The Lord watches over you—the Lord is your shade at your right hand;
    the sun will not harm you by day, nor the moon by night.
The Lord will keep you from all harm—he will watch over your life;
    the Lord will watch over your coming and going both now and
    forevermore.

Daniel Bacon, leadership consultant at Overseas Missionary Fellowship (OMF), provides us with one last reminder: "Technological developments have provided many helpful tools for missionary work, along with organizational structures that greatly facilitate the recruitment, sending, maintenance, and support of mission personnel. But . . . tools and organizations can never substitute for God's power, which comes alone in answer to prayer . . . dependence upon God in prayer is the ultimate way for doing spiritual work."[18]

Before you is the exciting ministry of fundraising. By now, you have not only developed positive feelings, you are also acquiring necessary skills. But before reading any further, put down the book, slow down your pace, and shut off—as well as possible—all outside distractions. Take time to talk with your heavenly Father. Acknowledge your need of His guidance, and ask for His provision as you undertake this special ministry.

CHAPTER 24

God Is Faithful

We have sought to carefully lay out a strategy based on real-life fundraising experience, but you must realize that the Lord works beyond our strategies.

Some years ago Torrey Johnson, founder of Youth For Christ, visited Inner City Impact for the first time. We spent the day together as he toured our facility and ministered to our staff. That afternoon we sat in my car outside the ICI headquarters, and he said, "Bill, tell me about the miracles. I want to hear about the miracles of this ministry."

When I began the ministry of Inner City Impact we had no money, no staff, and no building. We literally started on a sidewalk. I sold pots and pans to earn a living, but I knew God had a call on my life and we needed to reach out to these inner-city kids. As the story goes, we got the use of a union hall free of charge. At one point, we wanted to get that facility for our very own. Our efforts stalled, and yet we were able to stay there and use it temporarily to minister to kids. Then we set our sights on another facility, just two blocks away. We didn't have the funds, but we prayed earnestly that the Lord would provide $10,000 to enable us to get serious about our very own building. We put a deadline on the request and prayed that the Lord would provide $10,000 by December 25 of that year.

On December 21, I received a phone call. We had still been operating out of the old union hall. The one-and-only staff member serving with me called and told me to get down to the building as quickly as possible. The whole building was on fire. Word quickly spread through the Christian community in Chicago: "Have you heard that Inner City Impact has been burned out?" In my heart and mind, I was wondering how in the world the Lord would ever get us through this. Despite the fire, we still kept on praying for that $10,000.

I'd previously committed to take our Inner City Impact young people to camp in southern Wisconsin. On December 27, the buses pulled behind that burned-out building and loaded the kids to take them to winter camp. I figured we'd take the kids to camp, bring them back to Chicago, drop them off, and that would be the end of Inner City Impact. But God had something different in mind. While at winter camp I received a call from the one staff person left in Chicago to answer the phone and collect the mail. The person shared the exciting news that someone had sent in a check for $10,000. It was right to the penny, and right within the time frame we had prayed. God was faithful and working above and beyond our strategy. The amazing thing is that I had never met this man before, he had never given to our work before, and he had not even heard about the fire. God had prompted him to provide the gift.

I'm sure you'll have no fires and lost buildings to share in your life's story, but I'm confident you will have your very own stories of God's faithfulness.

I pray and look for those gifts that come in without any trace of my fingerprints—gifts that have not been made possible through my efforts, but by God's work alone. So work your plan as if it all depends on you, but knowing that in reality it all depends on Him.

> *Work your plan as if it all depends on you, but knowing that in reality it all depends on Him.*

Remember that prayer activates a powerful God. It unleashes His resources to accomplish His purposes. Prayer shows how inadequate we are and brings a heart full of praise back to the author and finisher of our faith.

Psalm 44:3 states, "It is not by their sword that they won the land, nor did their arm bring them victory; it was your right hand, your arm, and the light of your face, for you loved them."

Remember, it is not your ministry. You and I are merely on assignments from the Lord Himself. Let nothing deter you from getting the funds to impact your world for Christ.

God can do anything, you know—far more than you could ever imagine or guess or request in your wildest dreams! He does it not by pushing us around but by working within us, His Spirit deeply and gently within us. (Ephesians 3:20, THE MESSAGE)

May the Lord bless your People Raising efforts.

NOTES

Chapter 1: The Benefits of Raising Funds

1. Daniel W. Bacon, "The Tin-Cup Image Can Be Shattered," *Evangelical Missions Quarterly* 22, no. 4 (October 1986), 376.
2. Bud Taylor, *Taking the P.U. out of Deputation* (self-published pamphlet, Source of Light Ministries).
3. Scott Steele with Tom Frieze, International Missions (Reading, PA).

Chapter 2: The Biblical Basis for Raising Funds

1. Position paper on financial policy of the American Missionary Fellowship (Villanova, PA: AMF).
2. Serving In Mission materials (Charlotte, NC: SIM.) Used by permission.
3. Ibid.

Chapter 3: Yes, It Is Okay to Ask for Funds

1. Joel Darby, deceased.
2. Serving In Mission, "A Miraculous Way to Function," *Africa Now*, November/December 1976, 15.
3. Don W. Hillis, "Are Missionaries Beggars?" (Carol Stream, IL: The Evangelical Alliance Mission).
4. George and Donald Sweeting, *Lessons from the Life of Moody* (Chicago: Moody, 2001), 101–107.

Chapter 4: Confronting the Fear Factor

1. Donna Wilson, "Overcoming Emotional Barriers in Fundraising," handout. Funding Your Ministry Symposium, March 2, 2011, InterVarsity Christian Fellowship. Reprinted with permission of InterVarsity Christian Fellowship/USA. Copyright 2011 by InterVarsity Christian Fellowship/USA.
2. Ibid.
3. Ibid.
4. Betty Barnett, *Friend Raising* (Seattle: YWAM Publishing, 1991), 59–62.

Chapter 5: It's Really Not About You

1. Quoted in Steve Shadrach, *View Points* (Fayetteville, AR: BodyBuilders Press, 2010), 154.
2. Randy Alcorn, *The Treasure Principle* (Colorado Springs: Multnomah, 2008), 121–31.
3. Chip Ingram, *The Genius of Generosity* (Madison, MS: GenerousChurch, 2011), 36.
4. Ibid., 11.
5. Ibid., 14.
6. Ibid., 34.
7. Ibid., 42.
8. Ibid., 55.

Chapter 6: The Number One Enemy of Fundraising

1. Curtis Kregness, "The Enemy of Deputation Was Me," *Evangelical Missions Quarterly* (October 1986).

Chapter 11: Step 4: Get the Word Out

1. Taken from *MAF Ministry Partnership Manual* (Nampa, ID: Mission Aviation Fellowship). Used by permission.
2. Ibid.

Chapter 12: Step 5: Make Appointments

1. Mission Aviation Fellowship of Canada, *Support Team Development Manual* (Guelph, ON: MAF Canada, 1989). Used by permission.
2. Mission Aviation Fellowship, *Ministry Partnership Manual* (Redlands, CA: MAF), 271. Used by permission.

Chapter 13: Step 6: Conduct the Visit

1. Mission Aviation Fellowship of Canada, *Support Team Development Manual* (Guelph, ON: MAF Canada, 1989). Used by permission.
2. Dennis Carlson, Send International. Big Picture presentation.
3. MAF of Canada, *Support Team Development Manual.*
4. Ellis F. Goldstein, Ministry Partner Development, Campus Crusade. Used by permission.
5. Ibid.
6. Mission Aviation Fellowship, *Ministry Partnership Manual* (Redlands, CA: MAF), 271.

Chapter 15: Step 8: Say Thank You

1. Wycliffe Partnership Development.
2. Adapted from Sandy Buschman, 1995, material adapted from Ken Williams' "Fifty Ways of Expressing Gratitude," Wycliffe Bible Translators. www.chialpha.com/files/50waystosaythanks.pdf.

Chapter 17: Step 10: Expand Your Contacts

1. "Key Person Concept," Steve Rentz, *New Staff Support Team Development Training Manual* (Campus Crusade, 1991).

Chapter 18: Step 11: Cultivate Your Donors

1. Steve Rentz, *New Staff Support Team Development Training Manual.*
2. Pioneers, Orlando, FL, www.pioneers.org.
3. H. Brade and Alan J. Antin, *Secrets from the Lost Art of Common-Sense Marketing* (Chicago: Precept Press).
4. Steve Rentz, *New Staff Support Team Development Training Manual.*
5. Pioneers, Orlando, FL, www.pioneers.org.
6. Adapted from materials used by Regions Beyond Missionary Union.

7. Ken Williams, Wycliffe Bible Translators.
8. Scott Morton, *Raising Personal Support: A Biblical Approach to Fund Raising*, video seminar (Colorado Springs: NavPress).
9. Wycliffe Bible Translators.
10. Support Manual (Reading, PA: International Missions).
11. Thomas J. Peters and Robert H. Waterman, Jr., *In Search of Excellence* (New York: Harper & Row, 1982), 157–59.

Chapter 22: Coaching Can Make the Difference

1. *Merriam-Webster* online, www.merriam-webster.com.
2. Ibid.
3. Ellis Goldstein, Ministry Partner Development, Campus Crusade. Used by permission.

Chapter 23: The Role of Prayer in Fundraising

1. Steve Shadrach, *View Points* (Fayetteville, AR: BodyBuilders Press, 2010), 17–18.
2. Ernest Gambrell, *The Ministry of Deputation* (Memphis: Fundamental Baptist World-Wide Mission, 1987).
3. Bud Taylor, *Taking the P.U. out of Deputation* (self-published pamphlet, Source of Light Ministries).
4. Pioneers, Orlando, FL, www.pioneers.org.
5. Gambrell, *The Ministry of Deputation.*
6. From ministry materials provided by Greater Europe Mission (Monument, CO), www.gemission.org.
7. Ibid.
8. Missionary Tech Team, "Guide for Prayer," www.missionarytechteam.org.
9. Discussions of prayer/advisory group is adapted from materials from Wycliffe Bible Translators.
10. Ibid.
11. Ibid.
12. Ibid.
13. Ibid.
14. Ibid.
15. Ibid.
16. Ibid.
17. Ibid.
18. Daniel W. Bacon, *From Faith to Faith: The Influence of Hudson Taylor on the Faith Missions* (Littleton, CO: OMF Books, 1984), 185–86.

Acknowledgments

I would like to express thanks to some of the people who have been instrumental in making this revision a reality.

Special thanks to Greg Thornton, senior vice president of media at Moody Bible Institute. It was Greg who caught the vision many years ago for coming alongside missionaries, church planters, and ministries to provide tools to help them in this most critical area of fundraising.

Thanks to Dave DeWit, director of product management at Moody Publishers, for republishing *People Raising* and providing oversight in the update.

And special thanks to Annette LaPlaca, editor for Moody, who was a joy to work with and did a masterful job of making *People Raising* reader-friendly.

Thanks to my faithful administrative assistant, Edith Greaves. More important than her title is her ongoing prayer support for me, my family, and the ministries of Inner City Impact and People Raising.

And thanks to the many followers of People Raising who have shared their stories of God at work through their fundraising experiences. It is my privilege to connect with many of them.

About the Author

William Paul Dillon is a third-generation missions leader. His family began ministering in Chicago's inner city in 1918. Bill is married and has three grown children.

Bill is the founder and executive director of Inner City Impact, which ministers in Chicago's inner city and brings hope to the children, youth, and families who live there.

Bill's education includes a B.A. in Bible theology, Moody Bible Institute, Chicago; a B.S. in business administration, Elmhurst College, Elmhurst, Illinois; and an M.B.A from Murray State University, Murray, Kentucky.

In addition to administrative and teaching skills, Bill has written two books on basic Bible doctrine for children. He has spoken on more than twenty-five college campuses, in churches, and for Christian ministries.

Bill has served on the boards of the Moody Bible Institute Alumni Association, the Association of North American Missions (former chairman), and AWANA Clubs, International.

In 2005, Bill was honored by Moody Bible Institute as Alumnus of the Year.

Experienced in raising funds for nearly forty years and as founder and executive director of Inner City Impact, Bill has trained and coached numerous missionaries and knows well how to raise major gifts. He has conducted numerous fundraising seminars for various Christian ministries and associations. In our tight economy, Bill's ministry operates debt-free.

Bill writes from experience and continues to raise funds for the cause of Christ. He also is the founder and president of the People Raising ministry, which provides fundraising training for individuals and organizations. Training tools include a six-hour training program on DVD, CD, and MP3. He provides ongoing training through a monthly e-mail newsletter, blogs and conferences as well.

Fundraising Resources

DVD Resources

Dillon, Bill. People Raising, six-hour training program, www.peopleraising.com

Morton, Scott. Raising Personal Support, video seminar, Colorado Springs: NavPress, www.navpress.com.

Books

Alcorn, Randy. *The Law of Rewards*. Carol Stream, IL: Tyndale House, 2003.

_____. *Money, Possessions, and Eternity*. Carol Stream, IL: Tyndale House, 2003.

_____. *The Treasure Principle*. Colorado Springs: Multnomah, 2008.

Atkinson, Neil, *The Shrewd Christian: You Can't Have It All, but You Can Have More Than Enough*. Colorado Springs: Waterbrook, 2004.

Barnett, Betty. *Friend Raising: Building a Missionary Support Team That Lasts*. Seattle: YWAM Publishing, 2002.

Beisner, E. Calvin. *Prosperity and Poverty: The Compassionate Use of Resources in a World of Scarcity*. Eugene, OR: Wipf & Stock, 2001.

Blomberg, Craig L. *Heart, Soul, and Money: A Christian View of Possessions*. Joplin, MO: College Press, 2000.

Blue, Ron. *Generous Living: Finding Contentment Through Giving*. Grand Rapids: Zondervan, 1997.

Burkett, Larry. *Debt-Free Living: How to Get Out of Debt (and Stay Out)*. Chicago: Northfield Publishing, 2001.

Ingram, Chip. *The Genius of Generosity*. Madison, MS: GenerousChurch, 2011.

MacDonald, Gordon and Patrick Johnson. *Generosity*. Alpharetta, GA: National Christian Foundation, 2008.

Morton, Scott. *Funding Your Ministry: Whether You're Gifted or Not*. Colorado Springs: Dawson Media, 2007.

Shadrach, Steve. *Viewpoints: Fresh Perspectives on Personal Support Raising*. Fayetteville, AR: BodyBuilders Press, 2010.

Sommer, Pete. *Getting Sent: A Relational Approach to Support Raising*, Downers Grove, IL: InterVarsity Press, 1999.

Stanley, Andy. *Fields of Gold*. Carol Stream, IL: Tyndale House, 2004.

Willmer, Wesley K. *Revolution in Generosity*. Chicago: Moody, 2008.

Resources to Help with Giving and Money Management

Ronald Blue & Company
www.ronblue.com
800-841-036

Crown Financial Ministries
www.crown.org
800-722-1976

Eternal Perspective Ministries
(includes articles by Randy Alcorn)
www.epm.org
503-663-6481

The Gathering
www.thegathering.com
903-509-9911

Generous Giving
www.generousgiving.org
423-755-2399

The Stewardship Alliance
www.stewardshipalliance.com
812-386-9170

National Christian Foundation
www.nationalchristian.com
800-681-6223

The Timothy Plan
www.thetimothyplan.com
800-681-6223

Stewardship Partners
www.stewardshippartners.com
800-930-6949

BILL DILLON HAS SO MUCH MORE TO SHARE

He offers even more practical examples and answers many other questions that you will have as you engage in fundraising. Whether it be through his FREE monthly newsletter, tip of the month, blog, DVD, CD, MP3, or a live conference, you will be better equipped to raise needed funds. Take advantage of our 20% discount.

www.PeopleRaising.com/prb

- FREE monthly E-Newletter
- Register for People Raising Conference
- Additional training materials available on books, DVD, CD, & MP3
- People Raising blog

REVOLUTION IN GENEROSITY

HOW CHRISTIAN MINISTRIES CAN IMPLEMENT
THEIR SPIRITUAL FORMATION RESPONSIBILITIES
FOR HEARTS, MONEY & GIVING

Revolution in
GENEROSITY

TRANSFORMING STEWARDS
TO BE RICH TOWARD GOD

WESLEY K. WILLMER, EDITOR
FOREWORD BY CHARLES COLSON

978-0-8024-6753-9

Also available as an ebook

As Wes Willmer writes, generosity is the natural outcome of God's transforming work in individuals when they are conformed to the image of Christ. Fundraising and giving are not simply drops in the bucket. Capital campaigns and raising funds go deeper than the money. They are spiritual activities in becoming more like Christ.

MOODY
PUBLISHERS

www.MoodyPublishers.com